You can always tell when someone knows [...]
engaging, reflective and wise, but that's be [...]
a chaplain - years of working and walking [...]
understanding and being present in an insti[...]
Sector Ministry, Katy has made this experience available to hundreds or other chaplains
- and now it's available to you, too, through this book. I commend it very highly, and I
continue to thank God for Katy's faithfulness and commitment, both in living this ministry
and in sharing its lessons with others.

Paul Bayes, former Bishop of Liverpool

No day is ever the same in prison despite the routine and order. Katy demonstrates in this
book that prison life is varied and complex and ministering into this context is challenging.
Katy does this by telling stories about the people she spent time with and walked alongside
in her ministry as a prison Chaplain – real life people come into focus and we get to know
them in a way that is gospel-like. As we glimpse into the lives of those Katy has met in
prison we pause and are able to reflect on how we might know more about our God who
knows and loves each of us in all our beauty and brokenness.

Rev Canon Dr Ellen Loudon, Director of
Social Justice & Canon Chancellor, Diocese of Liverpool

Considering prison chaplaincy? This book is a massive encouragement and a must-read for
an insight into how life really is in there. It is the multi-tool Swiss army knife of Christian
Prison Ministry in all of its flavours, colours and textures. We as Chaplains become the
human face and listening ear on arrival through to the days of joyous release, hoping
never to return…
Katy describes one God ordained meeting after the next, unlocking Jesus in prison as we
are encouraged to in scripture. She brings alive what it is to follow this command, step
by step in the power of the spirit. Whilst the highs and lows of ministry in a chaotic, often
toxic setting can take its toll, this book continually reminded me of why I first said yes.

Rev'd Cliff McClelland, Anglican Chaplain, HMP/YOI Winchester

The role of a prison chaplain is so very valuable and most often gets little recognition. They can feel hurt, abused and used. This book tells how Katy kept going, praying and giving, doing what Jesus asked us to do in Matthew 25:39, "When did we see you sick or in prison and go to visit you?".

Katy looked beyond her own self and dedicated her life to helping those that the world so easily writes off. I know with my own life: when nobody cared, Jesus cared and showed it through people. This is exactly what Katy has been doing.

I would recommend you read this thought-provoking book and to pray for our chaplains. Thank you, Katy.

Gram Seed, author, CEO & Founder of Sowing Seeds Ministries

Heartbreak, Hope and Holy Moments: Insights from a Prison Chaplain

Katy Canty

Heartbreak, Hope and Holy Moments: Insights from a Prison Chaplain

WAVERLEY ABBEY
RESOURCES

Concept development and editing by Waverley Abbey Resources.

Design and typesetting by Nord Compo.

Paperback ISBN: 978-1-78951-428-5
eBook ISBN: 978-1-78951-429-2

To all the prisoners amongst whom I walked and who shared your lives with me. My prayer is that if you recognise yourself in this book, (though all names have been changed to preserve anonymity), you will know that you taught me so much about being in prison and hope beyond the walls.

A note from the author to all who read this book:

This book is about prison and from it you may understand more of what prison is really like, who prisoners really are and what is the role of Chaplaincy within it. But my prayer is that you will not only learn from it but it will inspire you to think through your own reactions. As you consider the questions at the end of each chapter maybe on your own or in a group, may you prayerfully analyse your own responses and how they may change as you gain a better understanding of life 'inside' and 'outside' the walls.

About Katy Canty

Born in London, raised in Tunbridge Wells, Katy attended University and Teacher Training College in York. Katy taught Biology in secondary schools in Hertfordshire for many years before marrying and moving to Liverpool.

She has always been involved in the Anglican Church and with a young family became involved primarily in children's work which continued for several years, but increasingly she felt called to minister to adults so put herself forward to become a Reader. As part of her training, she undertook a placement in a local prison – and never left, immediately aware that this was the place to which God was calling her. Expecting fear as she entered this unknown territory, she found instead an unexpected gift of compassion which remained with her in the succeeding fourteen years she worked there. During that time, she was ordained, and in the last few years became the Chaplaincy Manager responsible for a multi-faith team.

After retirement she continued to champion the importance of Chaplaincy within the Diocese and became the Dean of Sector Ministers, taking on the pastoral care of all the many and varied Chaplaincies. She has worked to establish and strengthen increasing connections between them and the local church, and continues to encourage more participation by volunteers willing to work in this 'outer edge' ministry to reach people outside the church walls and offer them the care and compassion of Christ.

In her spare time, she enjoys all forms of needlework, furnishing dolls' houses and watercolour painting.

Contents

PART ONE
The Common Round, the Daily Task

PART TWO
Grappling with Issues

PART THREE
Moving On

Foreword

Chaplains have always played an important role in society as they 'face the world' as representatives of not only the Church, but of Christ Himself (2 Cor 5:20). Recent years have seen a dramatic expansion of chaplaincy ministry within a whole range of contexts, with many organisations recognising the need for someone to minister into the emotional, physical, relational and spiritual lives of their people. In addition to chaplains within prisons, the NHS, and the armed forces, chaplains are now serving in shopping centres, gymnasiums, city centres, GP surgeries, and many other settings.

In my day-to-day role, as someone who trains students in a range of chaplaincy contexts, I read a lot of books, good books. Books about the theology of chaplaincy, models of chaplaincy, the impact of chaplaincy, amongst other things. Yet there are some things that courses, and purely academic books cannot teach, things that only experiencing the ups and downs of ministry can. However, what is exciting about Katy's book, is that she has captured the highs and lows of her ministry as a prison chaplain, and packaged and presented them in such a way, so as to give us the 'inside track' of her vast experience.

Every chapter is augmented with stories of real people that Katy has had the privilege to serve and minister to. As I read each account, I felt I was sat in the cell, stood by the prison hospital bed, holding someone's hand in the prison chapel. Katy masterfully recounts life stories of despair to hope, pointless to purposeful, captivity to freedom. Yet having said this, Katy does not simply celebrate the good news stories, she is honest enough to reflect on times of heartbreak, ongoing tragedy, and times when people gave up the fight in this life.

With raw honesty, Katy opens up her ministry experiences, her doubts, fears, sense of failure and triumphs, with the challenge that somehow, God was at work through it all, if only we could have the eyes to see and the ears to hear Him.

If you are an experienced chaplain, I pray this book will encourage you to see what God is still up to within your ministry context, and that it will remind you why you first said 'yes' to doing what you do. If you are just starting your chaplaincy adventure, in whatever context, I pray this book will spur you on to make a difference wherever He has placed you – just like Katy did.

Keith Foster
Head of Chaplaincy
Waverley Abbey College

Introduction
Not Quite What I Expected

> I was ill and you looked after me, I was in prison and you came to visit me.
>
> Matthew 25:36

The officer went ahead of me to open the cell door and I hung back, praying desperately about the prisoner inside. They had had to lock the prisoner up (which in those days was quite unusual) because he had been swearing uncontrollably and exhibiting bizarre behaviour on the unit. The officer said to me, 'Katy, he may swear at *you…*'. I thought this was a very sensitive concern, but one which I felt able to deal with. However, the fact remained, what could I possibly say to this man? As Chaplains, we are required to visit every new prisoner, check on their welfare and offer our services, but I wasn't sure how I would handle a possible torrent of violent abuse. I remember praying, 'God, what shall I say?' and just feeling the thought, 'Go in gently.' I knocked before entering and, before he had any time to speak, I said, 'Hello Aidan, I'm Katy and I've just come to see if you are all right.'

I entered the cell quietly and, to my amazement, did not get an immediate response. What I saw touched me to the core. Before me on the bunk was a man lying in the foetal position, whimpering like an animal. He seemed to be in such distress and beside himself. I spoke to him briefly and offered him our support if he wanted it and then left quietly. A few days later I found out that during an interview with the prisoner, the Manager and the officer, it had emerged that this man was in fact suffering from Tourette's Syndrome, a symptom of which is uncontrollable swearing, which would explain a lot of his frightening and unpredictable behaviour. He didn't remain in prison for long, but to this day that picture of such misunderstood distress has remained imprinted on my mind.

Simon was another prisoner who had been locked up before I was asked to see him. He was someone well known to us as he had been in prison several times. He was the very epitome of the 'angry young man', and actually quite frightening when his temper was aroused, which was a frequent occurrence. At that time, I did not know much about his drug addiction or his broken background, but the reason I was now being asked to see him was to bring him really bad news. Normally we would have asked the prisoner to go to the Manager's office when we break such news, where there is a degree of privacy but, in this instance, he was considered too violent and unstable to be allowed out. My task was to tell him that his mother was seriously ill. How would he react? Would he vent his anger on me? How would I deal with his violence? I remember praying desperately outside the cell and entering with a real sense of trepidation, while officers waited outside in case he 'kicked off'. As I began to explain the situation there was no violent response. Instead of being shouted at, he listened to me and was polite and reasonable. It was as though there was a stillness in that cell offering him inner strength, which enabled him to react without resorting to violence. I do not remember the exact turn of events at that time, but his mother did eventually die whilst he was still in prison. He always remembered that time when I came to see him and made reference to it years later. I expected violence and abuse but instead found acceptance and gratitude.

One of the men who had taken another's life wasn't quite what I expected either. I received a phone call one Sunday afternoon when I had only been working in prison for a few months. Stephen was in the Care Suite in Healthcare, and although this was not his first sentence, he was deeply distressed. The nurse who rang added, 'He's here because he killed his girlfriend.' That short walk from Chaplaincy to Healthcare saw me in turmoil. Nothing could prepare me – there wasn't really a manual on how to deal with situations like this. What would he be like? My vision of a murderer was a really scary, large hulk. Would I be safe with him? How could I offer him any support after he had done something so dreadful?

The Care Suite is where prisoners are put for a few days and nights who are considered to be at risk of suicide, and where they are also in the presence of other prisoner Carers who take it in turns to stay awake with them and speak and play games with them so the prisoner is never left alone. The room is furnished differently to a normal cell, with coloured curtains and duvet so that it looks more like a budget hotel room than a cell.

When I arrived, Stephen turned out to be quite large but not massive, and when I met him he was sitting on his bed and sobbing. I could not believe my eyes. He was so distressed and, over several more visits, told me his story of an argument with his girlfriend and the culmination when he had hit her. He hadn't meant to kill her and now he felt that he should not continue to live. He said that he wanted to be moved away from our prison because it was 'too nice', and he wanted to go to our local prison which was much less clean and modern. He also said that he wanted to hang himself and that he wished the death penalty was still in use because he felt that he had forfeited his right to life.

On that first occasion as he began to weep, I stood at some distance from him because I was still acutely aware that he had killed another female, but within me I sensed such a feeling of God's compassion for him as he sat so vulnerable and distraught, that eventually I plucked up courage to sit beside him on his bed and listen and respond to what he was saying. A few weeks later we sat together again – this time in the chapel. It was the day of the funeral of his girlfriend; the person he had so loved but also whose life he had taken. I remember weeping with him that day because I glimpsed again the utter desperation of this fellow human being; his remorse and regret and, above all, I felt a sense of the compassion that God felt for him and with him, in spite of what he had done.

Prison and the people in it were not at all what I expected. As I arrived the first time to visit I was amazed that it didn't really seem at all forbidding and the whole entrance to the building was a sea of beautiful flowers. Inside I was amazed at the Astroturf football pitch, more flower beds outside the units and even hanging baskets! The whole place resembled a holiday camp – although there was no one out to play in it. Even after all these years, the place is still kept clean and is always freshly painted. Every shred of litter is always removed so that it remains clean and decent. The units are not grey and drab but have brightly coloured doors and staircases. There are tables for snooker and table tennis, and everywhere is well-lit.

But if prison buildings are a bit of a surprise, how much more the prisoners who live there. Like many others, I had a sort of stereotype in mind of who I thought would be found in prison and what a typical prisoner would be like. If you read descriptions of prisoners in the press they are often dehumanised and described as inanimate 'scum' or at best 'beasts' or 'animals'. Yet when you meet prisoners, the most frightening thing about them is that they are apparently so 'normal' and often just like our neighbours and friends in their demeanour. I went into prison full of fear, but this was immediately supplanted by a deep sense of compassion, which was not my own but, in some way, drawn from the immense sea of compassion that is the love of God.

As I share with you the stories of some of those I have met, I hope that I will be able to show you a little of the reality of those who end up 'behind bars' and how, as I and my colleagues walk among them, it is as though we are walking in the footsteps of Jesus with them. It shakes our self-composure and it blows away so many of our pre-conceived ideas, because we have to face up to our own prejudices, our own fears and anxieties, our own doubts and our own real inabilities to love the unlovely and also challenge their behaviour.

Pause for reflection

What pre-conceived ideas do I have about people and their position before God? Am I willing to let go of my prejudices and carefully-worked-out theology when I encounter something or someone that doesn't quite fit my usual pattern of thinking? Am I willing to let go of fear and instead be filled with the compassion of God for the unlovely, even when my head is wanting to condemn them?

Prayer

Father God, may I be honest with You in the very depths of who I am. Lord, You know all my pre-conceived ideas and prejudices better than I do myself, and I want to give them to You for You to refine. Lord, fill me afresh with Yourself: Your compassion and patience especially for those from whom I would naturally recoil. Help me to be willing to be open to change and so become more like You and see people as You see them. Amen.

PART ONE

The Common Round,
The Daily Task

CHAPTER 1

Fleeting Encounters

Meeting prisoners on Induction
and other casual conversations

> The kingdom of heaven is like a man who sowed good seed in
> his field.
>
> Matthew 13:24

Every day (unless there is some sort of major crisis), the prisoners arrive at the chapel. Usually between fifteen and twenty men file in, sometimes noisily but more often in silence. Their faces are mainly masked and impassive, although occasionally one will break away from the group and greet one of us like a long-lost friend, as we recognise with sadness the return of one of our 'frequent fliers'.

Under the Prison Act (1952), there are only three people that are required to be present in order for a prison to function: a Director or Governor, a Medical Officer and a Chaplain. My position as a Chaplain is an interesting one therefore, as it means that much of the work carried out is what is described as 'statutory' – required in order to fulfil Prison Service Orders. In turn, this means that a Chaplain is required to be available 24 hours a day for 365 days of the year, and so one of us has to be on call day and night should our services be required. Every day there are specific duties that have to be undertaken irrespective of any other calls on our time. The three main duties required are to meet every prisoner on arrival in prison, to visit every prisoner in the Healthcare Unit and to visit every prisoner in the Care and Separation Unit. Technically speaking, we are also required to see every prisoner as they prepare to leave prison.

Daily we would hold our Chaplaincy Induction group in the Chapel, and insist that no matter how many times people had been in our prison before, they attend so that we could speak to them. Some days there would be a distinct air of hostility and resentment amongst those who had 'done it before' and who felt the need to air their belligerence as they arrived at the chapel. However, it never ceased to amaze me that, on most occasions, as we started to speak about what we could offer them, the men would listen most attentively and respectfully. We offered them our 'sacred space', which is the chapel itself and a smaller room across the corridor. The chapel was built for Christian worship and has an altar with a figure of the resurrected Jesus above it, and the stations of the cross around the walls. There is a rather fine icon picture which was donated, portraying Christ with arms outstretched above the city. On a Friday, the icon is covered, along with the stations of the cross, and the figure of Jesus is put behind a curtain, and then the space becomes a mosque. This room is increasingly also used for all sorts of other meetings and activities, as it is the only reasonably large space available in the prison, but as Chaplains we have worked very hard to ensure that, whenever possible, it is available for lads to come to just to sit and talk. There is something special about the chapel that I think is due to the fact that it is a 'prayed in' space. Somehow it is always a very quiet and peaceful place, an oasis for prisoners within the noise and chaos that is so much part of prison life. We always say to the lads, 'You probably think that you don't want anything to do with Chaplaincy. We know that most of you are not religious and probably don't know what you believe in, if anything, but this is a space for everyone and many prisoners do find themselves in the chapel at some point in their time here.' Understandably, most times that prisoners do come to chapel is on their 'sad' days: they come on birthdays (their own and often those of their children), on anniversaries and at times of funerals they are not permitted to attend.

After we have told the men about accessing services and groups, we speak to each one of them individually for just a few minutes. We ask each of them a few questions about themselves and their family network, not because we need to know, but because these few moments allow them to share with us not only immediate concerns, but also other issues, particularly bereavements and family problems. Seeing so many people daily, it can be easy for this to become a bit of 'conveyor belt system' for us, but for many of the prisoners, someone asking them about themselves and the people for whom they care is not something common to their normal life experience. Very early on in my time in prison, I remember a prisoner coming back to see me at the end of a day to say simply, 'Thank you for talking to me.' I was stunned, as I did not remember that I had said anything of outstanding wisdom or importance to him, but then I realised that, for him, a fellow human being expressing a vestige of interest in him as a person was unusual. Another prisoner thanked me for 'not shouting at him', and I saw that for many the concept of a civilised conversation and someone listening to them was also, sadly, an uncommon occurrence.

It is difficult to appreciate sometimes that the very smallest interest that we show someone can have the most amazing influence on a person who has never before experienced this. I remember Paul, who came to chapel every Sunday. Back then, I was still only a volunteer, but I made a point of speaking to him every week and asking him how he was. It was after only a few weeks that he came to me and said he had something for me. It was a little card with the poem on it, 'A cross in my pocket'. He said he wanted me to have it because 'I had taken him at face value'. I remember thinking, 'Hey, I'm the Chaplain; it should be me giving him this card, not him giving it to me!', but I was very touched by his action. I later learned his story and I will refer to it later, along with what happened next.

In our introductory talk in the chapel, we often speak about bereavements and offer our support to the prisoners if they have been bereaved themselves. As a consequence, quite of a few of those with whom we then speak will raise the losses they have had in their own lives. Time after time I have spoken to men whose eyes began to fill with tears at just the mention of parents or partners, and often stories would come spilling out, even though there were other prisoners within 'earwigging' distance. It seemed as though a gentle word was like releasing a pressure valve, and it was a relief for some of them to speak about loved ones. These brief encounters also seemed to open wide the possibility of facing up to issues that had previously been buried, either consciously or subconsciously, and I often had return visits from those with whom I had engaged briefly on Induction. To my shame, I often did not recall the details of their initial conversations, but chaplains always seem to be remembered and trusted, and the men remembered what they had said to me. Later in this book I will explore this further.

'Every little helps' is a popular slogan, but true of many of our encounters on Induction and beyond. The moments are often fleeting and routine, and yet even if we are able to help in just small ways, the lasting effect on some prisoners is well beyond the degree of our assistance. Rory had returned to prison after being released just a few days before. He had been instructed to get to a bail hostel in Liverpool, but instead had gone back to a Cheshire town, hence he had breached his bail conditions and been returned to jail. As he was not in his designated place, he had no accommodation and told me that he had spent the night sleeping in the public toilets in the town. In the morning, he had been seen by a neighbour of his father's, who told him that his father had in fact just died. Rory was overcome with desperation that he should get to his father's funeral. He had apparently gone and stood outside his brother's workplace all day in the hope of being able to find out when and where the funeral was to take place. He didn't dare enter the workplace as he had fallen out with his brother. He pleaded with me, 'Could you find out about the funeral?' I hesitated as I was not sure that I could find the relevant information when I had no more than his dad's name to go on, but decided to take up the challenge of contacting all the funeral directors in turn in what was fortunately a town rather than a city. It did not take long to not only find the appropriate funeral director but also, on chatting to him, to find out that he knew all about the family and its situation. I was able to pass on the detailed information to the Security Department and Rory was allowed to attend the funeral at very short notice. A few months later, Rory stopped me as I was doing my rounds. I had completely forgotten who he was, but he just stood there and said, 'I just want to thank you so much for getting me to my father's funeral.' I hesitated to take the credit for this as the decision about attending funerals lies not with Chaplains but with the Security Department, but he looked me in the face and said, 'I really mean that; thank you.' I found myself immediately engaging with him, asking about his brother, and he said they had hugged each other at the funeral. We talked a little more about him getting out of prison and getting his life back in order, but I sensed that the first step of healing and restoration had begun – because he had been able to pay his respects to his father even though he had been put back into prison.

One of the most startling examples of an Induction connection was Mikey. He had been in various prisons for a good part of his life. After our routine conversation, he asked for a book, which we offer them from a very small library we maintain. Due to the amazing generosity of various organisations, we have a few books in vast numbers, and daily offer copies to every prisoner to give them a constructive way of passing what can be very boring hours in cells. Mikey took the book *Why Forgive?*, by Johann Christian Arnold, which contains true accounts from people, some of whom could forgive and some of whom could not. I didn't think much of Mikey's asking for a book at the time, as this was a fairly routine request. However, a few days later, he bounced up to me on a Unit and told me he had read the book – and that he didn't agree with it. This was surprising on two counts: firstly, he had actually read the book and not binned it or otherwise disposed of it and, secondly, that he actually had an opinion about it. I asked him if he would like to discuss this further and he was keen to do so. We duly met for an hour in the chapel and he told me that he had two problems: one was that he could not believe that God could forgive him, and two was that he felt that he could not forgive others who had wronged him. He was clearly an intelligent man and I spent my time trying to convey my own understanding of the extent of God's love and forgiveness for him that would allow him to forgive others. He steadfastly refused to alter his opinion, but we parted on good terms and he took a Bible with him.

I didn't meet Mikey again for several weeks and then encountered him again in the Care and Separation Unit, where he had been sent after some misdemeanour on the Unit. He seemed very much less ebullient and did not engage much with me. However, after a few days he did start to speak to me and said he had been writing poetry, and I asked if he would show it to me. He gave me his work and I found that it was entitled 'Reflections', which was appropriate as he had written the whole thing as though he was writing in a mirror. All the letters were reversed, but once put before a mirror became clear to read. This was remarkable in itself, as prisoners are not allowed mirrors (in case they are used as offensive weapons), so he must have worked out in his mind how the letters would appear in a mirror. The gist of the poem was that as he looked into a mirror he saw himself and didn't like what he saw. All very interesting but again, I didn't really think much more about it. I went on leave for a few days and when I returned I found an amazing letter from him in my pigeonhole. In it he said that he had had an experience in his cell which he wanted to share with me. One night, as he was waiting for his tea, the Christian calendar which we also give prisoners, slipped down onto the table, so he picked it up and read it. These calendars are donated by an organisation that uses the King James Version of the Bible, so what he read was in slightly antiquated English, but the text was, 'How long willst it be before thou humblest thyself before me?' Mikey continued, 'I picked up your Bible [notice it is never theirs!] and it fell open at the very page of this text', so he started to read. Many of you will know that this is a quote from Exodus, and Mikey was astounded as he had just been writing a letter to his solicitor and he now found that this passage in the Bible was all about 'the law'. He read on and then described that suddenly he felt sure that God did forgive him and that he could forgive others – the two bones of contention that we had discussed at our meeting weeks before. But that was not quite the end. He said in his letter that because he knew I was away he would put his letter in the Bible and give it to an officer to give to me, as he thought he was going to be transferred to another prison. As I looked again at the envelope I saw that he had written a final comment on it. He said that when he went to get the letter to give to the officer, he found it was in the part of the Bible about David and Bathsheba and how God had also forgiven David. Mikey did get transferred and I never saw him again. One meeting after Induction had played a significant part in changing this man's life. Whether or not Mikey has been released from prison and been able to lead a law-abiding life, God alone knows, but I do believe that he was challenged in an unforgettable way.

Pause for reflection

If we have Christ within us, then every time we speak to someone, we can allow Christ within us to minister to them. Do I allow Christ to speak through me or am I too ready to present my own ideas and opinions?

Do I draw from Christ every day so that I am filled with His presence and able to reflect Him in all I say and do?

Many people we meet today we will never see again; am I praying blessing on all my casual encounters with people I meet on the street, on the bus, in the shop?

Prayer

Jesus, You had one-off encounters and conversations with so many people whom You never saw again and yet each one was left with a sense of Your presence and blessing. Please fill me afresh with Your Spirit so that in all the conversations I will have with both friends and strangers, You may minister Your love and encouragement. Amen.

CHAPTER 2

All in a Day's Work

Statutory visits to Healthcare and Care and Separation Unit

> He was despised and rejected by mankind, a man of suffering, and familiar with pain.
>
> Isaiah 53:3

After Induction, the next tasks of the day are always the same. We are required to visit every prisoner on Healthcare and in the Care and Separation Unit. The history behind this is that the Chaplain is seen as an independent observer and therefore required to make sure that there are no signs of any prisoners being ill-treated. In training I was told that we had to have every door opened to us to check there were no pools of blood on the floor!

In reality, we work closely with the very busy staff and make sure our daily presence is of use to them as far as we can. We are always guided by their knowledge of individual prisoners and, if we are told that men are too volatile or dangerous, we will follow their lead because the last thing we want to do is to cause any more disturbance to already stressed places.

Care and Separation Unit (CSU) used to be called Segregation or 'the Block', but its name was changed to give it a more therapeutic overtone. At the same time, the place itself was repainted from grey to brighter colours, and prisoners' works of art were displayed, which gave it the appearance of a slightly deserted gallery.

Prisoners who end up being sent here will be those who have infringed prison rules, such as being involved in fights or assaults, being found in possession of drugs or phones or generally exhibiting behaviour that is too volatile or unpredictable to be sustained on a regular Unit. Increasingly we are seeing prisoners who have taken Spice (Mamba) and who are therefore often violent and unpredictable. Every day there are adjudications and prisoners are transferred back to normal locations when they have served their allotted time of separation. However, some men do remain in CSU for a while, often awaiting transfer to another prison.

Our daily rounds are of a routine nature, and we are aware that many of the men do not wish to engage in long or deep conversations with a Chaplain, especially one they see day after day! But our presence is understood and I remember one man completely humbling me when he met me on a Unit one day saying, 'You came to visit me when I was in Seg.' I felt dreadful as I had no recollection of him and had probably only asked if he was 'OK', and yet the presence of a caring face must have made such an impression on him. And the fact that we visit them means that we are there if they need us; sometimes a man would ask me to bless him or, more often to come and light a candle with him on an anniversary, since it would be difficult for them to come over to the chapel as they are on restricted conditions. Probably the most memorable visit was when I was asked to light a candle with a very unstable and disturbed man. In fact, he was considered so dangerous that he was a 'five-man unlock' – something I have never seen before or since. Some of the men can have their doors opened by a single officer or most when two officers are present. If someone is particularly difficult, three men are required, but five men obviously indicated a very violent man. In addition to that, these officers were dressed in riot gear in case the man 'kicked off' and they had to come and rescue me. I remember being extremely nervous as I waited to go in to the cell, and with the usual sense that of myself I had nothing to give. However, when I entered the cell the prisoner was very polite and respectful, and we lit the candle and I prayed with him. It was an odd situation as I realised I stood as a woman with him alone whilst outside there were five hefty men poised to defend! I have to admit I did not prolong the encounter and escaped as soon as I could!

Because men in CSU have broken prison rules, they are often denied privileges. If their behaviour is very poor they lose everything including their personal possessions for the time they are there. However, they are allowed to have a Bible (or Qur'an) if they require one, and we are also allowed to give them faith litera-ture. In actual fact, many of the prisoners asked for Bibles whilst they were in CSU. There were probably many and varied reasons for this. The small Testaments provided by the Gideons were just the right size to act as Rizla papers for their 'smokes'. If they had no tobacco because they had lost their right to buy it, they might smoke their tea bags! We only hoped that maybe some of them might get to read the 'holy' Rizla paper as they rolled it! Many lads *did* read the Bible whilst in CSU as it was something to do. They also devoured Christian books that we gave to them – stories of other men who had got it all wrong, been to prison and found God and a new way of life. On at least two occasions men called me into their cells to speak to me in private and told me that after reading the book *The Cross and the Switchblade* by David Wilkerson, they had started to cry. One of them said, 'Miss, I got down by my bed and said, "God, please sort my life out".' In the stillness and the nakedness of solitary confinement, it seemed that God had become real for them. When everything was stripped away and they had nothing to distract them, they found God waiting there as He had always been.

It was to CSU that they brought Daniel. He was in a terrible state – deeply distressed and suicidal. He had taken a life, and felt so guilty and remorseful that he felt that his own life was not worth living. He had a chequered background – had struggled with education and had been bullied all his life. Now he had got into trouble in prison, hence his arrival in CSU. He was so profoundly suicidal that they took the ultimate step of putting him in 'strips' (a gown that is made of very tough fabric so that it cannot be torn into ligatures). He was put into the special cell which contains no fixtures or fittings to which ligatures could be attached. In essence, it contains a low-level concrete block and nothing else. Through his tears, Daniel cried that prison officers had taken away his rosary beads and that he needed them to sleep at night. The officers had removed them because the string of beads might also be used as a ligature. What I did bring him was a small card with a picture of the cross on it which we give to prisoners when they visit chapel for a bereavement. It had a bright blue background and Daniel attached it to the wall – possibly with toothpaste. In that dark grey cell, it was the only thing there and it seemed to me that it almost 'glowed' on the wall. I prayed with him and carried on praying that he would not attempt to take his own life. Years later, he told me that at the time he had had razor blades on him, but that after our prayer he had not used them and the picture 'got him through the night'. He has gone from strength to strength with therapeutic help.

The Healthcare Unit in prison contains twelve beds and is usually fully occupied. Here we tend to those who are ill physically and mentally. The pressure on accommodation here is enormous. Those who are physically ill do not remain here long, unless they are terminally ill or in the last stages. Many in the Unit are those with acute mental health issues. Ideally, they would not remain here long either, but the sad fact is that there is a massive waiting time to get anyone into more suitable outside institutions. And so we tend to those who are sick in so many different ways, and Chaplains make a daily visit to speak to each of these men.

We see some amazingly bad injuries that have often occurred before the men come into prison. Bones are broken when unsuccessful burglars really do fall off drainpipes! I remember one lad who told me he was running away from the police and jumped into what he thought was a canal to escape from them, but unfortunately it turned out to be the railway track and he had completely shattered most of his leg bones.

My first glimpse of Peter was a terrible sight. It was his first time in prison, and he was devastated at having committed a crime. He had decided to kill himself with a gun and had aimed it at his face. He arrived in prison with his jaw blown apart under his ear and in a state of deep shock. I felt great sympathy for him and said that I would ring his wife to reassure her that he was OK – Daniel was now very concerned about how she would be coping. Peter went through extensive bone surgery, with grafts being taken from his leg, and I often had a chat with him as he remained in Healthcare for months. I rejoiced with him when at last he was able relocate into a normal Unit when his treatment was complete. A year or so later, he was pleased to tell me that he was imminently being released and he just wanted to say thank you to me because I had rung his wife when he first arrived in prison. Again, this was something that had not really remained in my memory, but was another example of a fleeting action which meant so much to a prisoner.

Another badly fractured jaw belonged to a very sad man called Andrew. He had been in prison before and we had had a lot to do with him. First time round, he told us he was a Roman Catholic by background, and he began to attend Mass at the chapel. So faithful was he, that eventually he was baptised in prison by the priest so that he could receive Mass. He also came to our Bible study group and we spent time having conversations with him. He talked about his broken relationship with his girlfriend and the children that he loved so deeply. He appeared to want to make something of his life, hence his commitment to chapel, and he told me that he had tried to take his life on more than one occasion on the outside, but each time it had failed. I remember that he told me he tried to hang himself from a tree but the branch snapped. We thought he would make something of himself as he left prison but, in a few months' time, he was back. When I saw him I was absolutely shocked. Like Peter, Andrew's jaw was round the side of his ear, and his face was black and blue. It transpired that he had been in a fight, and his opponent had actually stamped on his face. His physical injuries were treated and his body recovered fairly speedily, but it seemed that his inner self had given up the fight. He stopped coming to chapel and we saw little of him. When we did speak to him, he was always ready to talk, mainly about his children, but a few months after he left prison he at last succeeded in what he had set out to do – he hanged himself to escape from all his inner turmoil and pain. I still have a poem that he wrote for the chapel.

The other aspect of Healthcare is that here we visit prisoners who are terminally ill and may be dying. I think of Jack, a young lad in his twenties, who was dying of a brain tumour. As far as I recall, he had no friends or family, and he never caused any problems – he was always quiet and respectful. As his condition deteriorated, he became almost blind and staff had to put a large sign on his door so he could make out which was his cell. He went downhill quite fast but was cared for so compassionately by the Healthcare staff. When he died, we had a memorial service for him in the chapel and the staff who had cared for him in Healthcare came and wept; touched at the sadness of the loss of such a young life, whatever his offence.

With an aging population, in prison we are seeing more and more elderly men who will die whilst they are with us. Although his background was Roman Catholic, Frank preferred to attend Church of England services, and was a regular chapel attender. He was a historic sex offender and had a fairly lengthy sentence. He also came to the Discovery Group that I held on his Vulnerable Prisoner Unit. For a long time, he said very little but seemed to be growing in faith and was reading his Bible and praying. In the group, we study different courses and had used the Alpha course. As Frank was in prison for so long, he was still there when I went to repeat Alpha. One evening at the end of the session he quietly shared with the group that on the previous run-through of the course he had prayed the prayer that Nicky Gumbel spoke on the video, and he felt he could 'let go' of his past and had found 'real peace within'. This was borne out by his attitude to life and other prisoners, by whom he was loved and respected. His health gradually faded and he came to Healthcare. I was able to pray with him and he passed away peacefully. He had a Catholic funeral on the outside. We had a memorial service inside, which was well attended by his fellow prisoners, and the accolades he received from them were very touching. Undoubtedly, his quiet presence and kindness had spoken to many of them and he had found peace deep within, despite his surroundings.

Brian also attended chapel regularly as a staunch member of the Church of England. He had attended a church on the outside and I had a phone call from his incumbent who was very supportive. During the course of the conversation, the incumbent mentioned that his church identified as a 'Forward in Faith' church, and therefore he thought it unlikely that Brian would receive Communion from a woman. I decided that I would speak to Brian, and we actually got on very well. He also came to chapel and did receive Communion from me. He had a terminal condition before he came to prison and again his health deteriorated quite rapidly. In an amazing way, one Sunday when he was too weak to attend chapel, he had requested Holy Communion and I took it to him and anointed him with oil. Two hours later he had died, much to the surprise of the Healthcare staff who had not expected him to go so quickly. It also fell to me to accompany the Family Liaison Officer to visit the family to tell them of Brian's death, and it was so comforting to be able to tell them that virtually the last thing that he had done in his life was to receive Communion.

Not all those who die want to have Chaplaincy involvement and we respect both theirs and their families' wishes. As so many of the prisoners we see register themselves as 'Nil' religion as they go through Induction, we are sensitive that they may not wish to have any specific ministry, but sometimes the families of such men do have faith and at this point in life are grateful and wish to have some kind of closure in a spiritual way.

Pause for reflection

It may be that only when everything is stripped away and we see ourselves as we really are that we see the true extent of God's mercy for each one of us. Am I open to letting God see me as I really am – warts and all – and to accept the love and grace that he wants to give to me?

Am I open to receive God's healing, not only of body but also of spirit?

Can I find God in the dark and difficult places of my life as well as when times are easier?

Prayer

Loving Father, thank You so much that You are always there, ready for us to turn to and find You.

As I go through dark and lonely times, may I know the light of Your presence. When I go through painful times, may I know the strength of your love. When I go through times of doubt and uncertainly, may I know the power of your protection. Amen.

CHAPTER 3

Potpourri

The diversity of the Chaplaincy role in a multi-faith, ecumenical environment

> When he saw the crowds, he had compassion on them, because
> they were harassed and helpless, like sheep without a shepherd.
>
> Matthew 9:36

When one tries to describe a typical day in the life of a Chaplain, really there is no such thing. From the moment one arrives in the morning, very early, until the time one leaves, the day is normally crammed full from beginning to end, because so much of our work is as a direct response to immediate need. Most of the requests we receive from the Units to visit prisoners are due to very grave situations in their lives, so most of our conversations with the prisoners are when feelings are very raw and they are often distressed. And yet there may be no time to recover from one such encounter before one is thrust into another. I remember one morning when I had recorded in the Chaplaincy journal, 'Death of two babies before 8am.' Two members of the outside community had rung in to give details of bereavements and, in both cases, had asked us to tell the prisoners concerned. Apart from attempting to reassure and support the caller and the practicalities of checking the information, the emotional strength required to face two separate lads with such bad news and to support them as they reacted was very demanding indeed – but that had to be done alongside all the other statutory requirements of that day with little time to pause in between. Apart from the emotional side, the whole procedure for dealing with such happenings has to be logged and relevant staff informed so that, for example, provision can be made for the prisoner to attend the funeral if that is considered to be appropriate. Over the years, the amount of administrative work for each encounter has increased by an enormous degree, and we are required to document everything in several different places.

Chaplains rarely have any kind of administrative assistance, and so they often spend an amazing number of hours sitting at computers inputting information. It also means that we are responsible for all our own ordering, processing and general maintenance! On one day, I recorded that during my time in prison I had dealt with the organisation of a year's supply of diaries and calendars, the ordering of prayer mats for our Muslim prisoners, and the measuring up of the windows in the chapel for new curtains, as well as getting out the Christmas crib and tree decorations. I had spoken to one of our sessional Chaplains about a problem with his monthly pay, and to a fellow Chaplain who was looking for a sessional faith Chaplain in their establishment and wanted to share ours, and to our Senior Manager about a new TV – and dispensing with the old one. I had typed up lists of Welsh-speaking prisoners wishing to attend their own carol service and collated lists of visitors for the Community Carol Service. I had been over to speak to a Unit Manager about ensuring that a Christmas tree was put out on their Unit as the prisoners were threatening unrest if they didn't get one! In between all this I carried out all the statutory duties and carried out an Assessment, Care in Custody and Teamwork (ACCT) Assessment on a Sikh in Healthcare and spoke to a lad who was feeling under threat on another Unit. This just illustrates the complete potpourri of tasks that come our way!

We are an ecumenical, multi-faith team, and work closely together. In the latter years of my time as a Chaplain, I became the Chaplaincy Manager, but before that time we had merely functioned as individuals within a team. Only three of us were employed full time, so the other nine or ten came in from time to time. As the number of faith adherents to other world faiths were fairly small, these Chaplains came in only once a week or less, and so the organisation of their requirements and festivals tended to fall to those of us who were constantly in prison. This made for good relationships between us and I learned a lot from these faith partners. I remember one of these Chaplains once saying, 'We all try and give the lads some hope', which I felt was an amazing description of true multi-faith chaplaincy.

Apart from those particular interactions mentioned above, on many days we had so many encounters with individual prisoners that it was quite overwhelming. On another occasion, I recorded my day as follows:

After the Induction interviews, I was informed that Kevin's father had died and arranged for a compassionate visit in the Visits Hall for his sisters to come and tell him personally. He later came over to the chapel for a time of quiet and I rang his girlfriend on his behalf so that she could give us the funeral details as they became available. I then visited CSU, which had 21 prisoners there and many prisoners waiting for Adjudications, and therefore had very busy staff. I visited Alan who did not have anyone to visit him, and told him that I had an Official Prison Visitor for him now. These are volunteers who come in regularly to have a chat with prisoners in the Visits Hall and are a wonderful source of encouragement and support. Alan, a man still in his twenties, was serving a very long sentence and was very pleased indeed at the prospect of having a regular visitor. I also spoke to Chris who wanted to talk about spiritual things. He was a highly educated man with qualifications and was struggling with the education provision in prison because it was too basic. I prayed with him and suggested he pocketed his pride and retook his Level 2 qualifications as it would give him something to do! A phone call from a Manager asked me to visit Thomas on his Unit who was appearing very 'blank'. I managed to get out of him that he had lost his father, his mother had had a stroke, and he was detoxing from alcohol and anti-depressants. He then told me he was 'quite OK', but it had been interesting to talk and he would consider doing our Living with Loss course. I also went to see Paul who had put in an application to see a Chaplain because he had recently lost his grandmother and realised he probably wouldn't be allowed to attend the funeral. I chatted to him for a bit and suggested that he write something about his grandmother and come over to the chapel at the time of the funeral. The last visit of the day was to Trevor who was on an ACCT booklet. He had a broken arm but was refusing to take paracetamol because it didn't agree with him and had fallen out with the doctor over this. Clearly in pain, he had threatened to harm himself if his meds 'didn't get sorted'. This is a familiar story and one which requires wise handling, as the plea for painkillers has to be monitored carefully in light of other addictions. I finished the day by completing all the required paperwork which goes with such encounters!

Chaplaincy is certainly a very demanding job, both emotionally and spiritually but, at the same time, a privilege to stand alongside these men in their time of need. It is strangely satisfying and worthwhile.

Whilst many of our conversations are useful and hopefully productive, they are nearly always interspersed with other matters of less importance, and this is what makes up the fabric of Chaplaincy. On another day, I recorded:

> On one Unit I had six 'random' conversations when I went to check on lads on ACCT booklets. Zac wanted to find out the sex of the baby he was expecting. Stuart was making inquiries about his 'Mormon chocolate'. Adherents of The Church of the Latter Day Saints are not permitted any stimulants, so if they register themselves in prison as members of this faith, they have to be provided with an alternative to tea or coffee, such as chocolate. This is a well-known prison 'scam', so we get many registered Latter Day Saints who are not on the official register, but we have to allow them to follow their stated religion. Ben wanted to talk about the guilt he felt about the death of his twin sister who had been in a coma for three years, but he had missed her final passing and felt he had failed to get her away from her abusive boyfriend, resulting in her taking the overdose that produced the coma. Connor told me his father had just had a triple bypass and he wanted to sort out his life, but there were 'obstacles all the time'. Nick wanted some rosary beads and Daniel wanted to talk to me about his forthcoming appeal and said he would be in chapel on Sunday.

Every one of those lads needed to talk to someone, whether the matter was life-changing or trivial, and that is where a Chaplain can be just the person who, as one of my colleagues once said, is someone who 'sits where they sit' (see Ezek. 3:15). Whether or not lads remember what we have said to them or whether it makes any lasting effect, we very often do not know, but we feel that as we are in every part of prison we are a living presence and a reminder of God; maybe even the 'aroma of Christ' (2 Cor. 2:15). In a fast-changing prison, one often feels that every encounter we have is so fleeting and one rarely meets prisoners more than once, and yet who knows what the outcome of any one conversation may be? One lad came back to prison and said to me, 'I remember what you said to me when my nan died; it really changed my life.' 'But you're back in prison,' I replied. To which he responded, 'Yes, Miss, but only for a couple of weeks this time!'

We get used to dealing with slightly unusual situations and sometimes have to ensure that we take things in the right way, at the right time. I received a phone call one morning from Visits to say that they had received the news of the death of Humphrey's dad. As I pursued this to confirm it, I discovered that in fact the message had been misheard and the deceased was in fact a dog, called Sammy. In many respects, I was relieved and certainly glad that I had ascertained this before I went to give him the news. Actually, the death of his dog was probably more traumatic to this individual than that of his immediate family. Another lad came to the chapel to light a candle for Clive, which turned out to be his cat. I was sent over to a lad in CSU to give him the good news that he had just become a dad. I told the staff the name of the lad and they took me to a cell. Relieved to be the bearer of good tidings for a change, I burst in and shook him by the hand and said. 'Well done, you've just had a little boy.' The look on his face was indescribable; one of shock, horror and everything else in between. And then the officer realised he had taken me to the wrong cell and I had informed the wrong person, who apparently might also have had something to hide!

In our time on Units, we also spend time with other staff. Whilst many of them would not profess to having any kind of religious belief, they respect us and, as they get to know us, will often ask us about all sorts of things from solving 'religious' crossword puzzle clues, to why Christians believe in certain things. They also perceive that at times a Chaplain may be exactly what the prisoners need, even if the prisoners themselves may not see this. When an officer is dealing with a whole unit of men, he or she may not have the time to have an in-depth conversation with a prisoner who is feeling depressed, whereas a Chaplain has a bit more time – or at least has a degree of flexibility. Over the years, we have won the trust and respect of other staff. I have never ceased to be amazed at the wonderful team of Prison Officers and other staff, and the way in which we work together. Most of the people who come to work in prison have genuine care for the prisoners and a sense of 'wanting to make a difference'. As staff cuts have taken hold, the work has become much more challenging, especially with the growth of violence and the continued use of new psychoactive substances (NPSs), previously called 'legal highs'. As Chaplains, we always stand alongside staff and often act as a sounding board so that they can vent their anxieties and frustrations to an empathetic but neutral body. And, of course, the staff will have many other burdens that are common to all of us, bereavement, problems at home, long-term illness, care of their elderly relatives. As we take the time to listen to staff, we hope that in some small way we are supporting them so that they are better able to cope, not only with these situations, but also with the very emotionally exhausting work they carry out in prison.

Another facet in this theme of potpourri is the rather relaxed way we have to approach everything we organise in terms of faith. There is no room in prison for static procedures; things can alter suddenly and so can the format. Our weekly chapel services are dependent on the presence of Prison Officers, who may suddenly be called elsewhere and we may have to wait. We work around our prison day, which includes times when prisoners are locked up at set times. So if a prisoner wants to come to the chapel at the same time as a funeral on the outside, we may have to give or take an hour or so, to get to the nearest possible time. At Christmas, the Roman Catholic 'First Mass of Christmas', traditionally occurring about midnight, will be scheduled for 3pm in the afternoon. One year Hanukkah fell on Christmas Day and, as Hanukkah begins after daylight hours, we arranged for the single Jewish person to attend the chapel in the afternoon and closed the curtains so it felt darker! With limited spacing in the Chaplaincy rooms, we share our space and often negotiate with our Muslim colleagues to accommodate both Muslim prayers and Good Friday in the same space.

Probably the most bizarre service I helped to conduct was on Ash Wednesday. We had already had staff and prisoners over to the chapel for a very simple act of remembrance, but there were some prisoners and staff in Healthcare who were unable to attend. We therefore went straight over to that Unit, carrying all that we required for the service. The only room that is available there is their fairly small TV room, which has glass panels on the corridor side so we were very visible to all. We gathered an eclectic collection of staff and several prisoners, some of whom had acute mental health problems. As the service got under way, there was a bit of a movement outside in the corridor and, to my amazement, I was confronted with an enormous hawk which was being carried down the corridor by a prisoner. He was actually en route to visit a prisoner in Healthcare, as birds of prey are sometimes used in therapy to assist very vulnerable prisoners. The service limped on, subject to the frequent interruption by the questions and comments of one lad who was very mentally unwell. When we got to the part of the service called the 'giving of the ashes', I moved around to distribute ashes as a symbol of repentance. I said to the lad who had been asking many questions something along the lines of, 'Turn away from sin and be faithful to the Gospel', to which he replied in a very loud voice, 'I will.' I looked at the faces of the staff and realised that most of us wanted to laugh as it sounded as though he had just agreed to marry me! However, they all received the ashes and went back to their cells proudly wearing them on their foreheads, and I am sure that God understood that whilst our ceremony may not have had its customary gravitas, the hearts were at least willing!

One year the rabbi agreed to celebrate the Passover meal with us and a group of lads who attended our weekly Bible Study group, so that he could explain what each part of the meal meant. We liaised with the kitchen over a list of requirements, most of which were not standard prison issue, so they did what they could and substituted where necessary. The result was interesting to say the least. We had a very large bowl of parsley in great big chunks which was *karpas*, which might have been in salt water, and then dollops of horseradish sauce to serve as *maror* (bitter herbs) and dollops of stewed apple for *charoset* (chopped fruit, nut and wine dish). I don't remember there being any lamb at all (probably too expensive), but we did get hard boiled eggs for *beitzah*. It was just the overwhelming quantity of the parsley that was amazing. In search of unleavened bread, they had provided bagels, which unfortunately are leavened. However, not to be deterred, as our prisoners saw what they considered to be a meal in front of them, they wasted no time in devouring this rather austere concoction. One lad proceeded to cram as much of everything as he could into the bagel and eat it like a hamburger! Our rabbi very carefully explained all the stages of the Passover meal to them and we felt that, in spite of the culinary peculiarities, this had been a very helpful event for them. We were somewhat bemused and not a little perturbed to hear one of them, as he was leaving, ask the rabbi, 'Are you a Jew?'!

We may feel that anyone who has a faith really should not be in prison, if they have followed the ethical and moral precepts of that faith. It is amazing, therefore, that we do continue to receive lads who do profess faith, and we can only hope that in prison, as we reach out to them where they are on their journey, they come to a deeper understanding of faith. I believe that faith is a hugely important cornerstone to draw upon as the prisoners seek to rehabilitate and reshape their lives, allowing God to work in every part of their life.

Pause for reflection

How ready am I to respond to changes that happen to my normal routine?
How can I find God when things are not very orderly or organised?
How can we learn more about God from those who see things in a very different way to us?

Prayer

Loving Father, thank You that You made humans in Your own image and each one of us reflects You in a different way. Help us always to be open to seeing You in new ways and being willing to change and adapt as You continue Your formation within us. Amen.

Grappling with Issues

CHAPTER 4

Broken in Mind

Issues of mental health and its treatment

> ...they found the man from whom the demons had gone out, sitting at Jesus' feet, dressed and in his right mind; and they were afraid.
>
> Luke 8:35

I was warned to be very careful when I went to speak to Austin, as he was locked up but might not have any clothes on. He had been transferred to Healthcare from the Care and Separation Unit (CSU) as he was exhibiting bizarre and unacceptable behaviour. At that time prisoners who were in CSU were required to wear red tracksuits as a distinguishing feature so that they were readily recognisable as being potentially unpredictable or violent when being moved from place to place.

Austin was suffering from mental health issues that required monitoring in Healthcare, but was still under CSU conditions. Unfortunately, in his confused state, Austin had got it into his head that the red clothes were impregnated by the devil, and so he had taken them off and thrown them out of the window. Even when given clothes of a more standard grey, he still refused to wear them and they ended up in the same place. The day I went to see him, I was relieved to see that Austin was well-covered by bedding and appeared to be asleep – any verbal contact was likely to be incoherent and difficult. When he had first come to prison, he had engaged well with Chaplains and might have had some contact with church on the outside, possibly through the receipt of meals or shelter. He even came to chapel services from time to time. But he was a bit of a loner and was bullied by other prisoners who were ready to 'pick on' those who were a bit different. He came back to prison many times, and each time seemed to decline in health and strength. He finally passed away whilst he was in prison. I took his funeral so that he had the dignity of being given a personal 'send-off'. In the absence of any family, it was myself and three members of staff from the prison who formed the congregation. I suspect that most of his adult life had been in one form of institution or another, and maybe his slow decline was really a release.

Mental illness is a major problem in prisons. Although available statistics are difficult to find, the House of Commons Justice Committee in 2021 reported around 10% of prisoners were recorded as receiving treatment for mental illness with one suggestion that as many as 70% may have some form of mental health need at any one time. As far back as 1997 a report stated that nine out of ten prisoners had one or more psychiatric disorders – psychosis, neurosis, personality disorder, alcohol misuse and drug dependence – and 70% had two or more conditions. Whilst many might argue that drug dependence and alcohol abuse are separate issues, nevertheless the figure is high. And as prison population has continued to increase and drug addiction and alcoholism show no signs of abating, this will surely continue. It is well known that since the Care in the Community system was initiated the number of mentally ill people in the community has decreased in direct proportion to the numbers now found in prison. If a person is found wandering around acting in an unpredictable manner, it is difficult to know where he should be sent. One of the prisoners I met on Induction was very agitated and afraid and showing great signs of mental distress. It transpired that he had presented himself at an Accident and Emergency Department claiming that someone was out to kill him and that he had tied explosives round his waist – which he clearly had not. The police were called and one of them rang round all the local mental health hospitals – but there were no beds, so he was sent to prison with a charge of bomb hoax. He did receive mental health intervention once in prison and was soon returned to the community. We understand that increasingly men will be imprisoned who show severe mental health problems when they appear in court, because it is understood that once in prison they are more likely to get into the mental institutions that can help them.

Meanwhile, prison has to cope with a wide range of disorders, and the only place to care for those with severe problems is in Healthcare, which has only a small number of beds and needs also to cater for those with physical difficulties. As Chaplains, we daily visit these very sick people and get to know some of them very well. Sometimes they are so ill that it is difficult to establish any communication with them. When I spoke to Dieter, who was hiding behind a mattress on his toilet, I remember being so pleased when he stood up and spoke to me! Although the depth of our engagement with those who are so ill may be bizarre or limited, often they do respond to us. Peter wanted me to bless him before he went off to be sectioned, and Joel sang to me! On a darker note, when I prayed with Michael, he joined in with gibberish.

In their dark places, these men often seem to get quite mixed up with spirituality, and religious mania may well be symptomatic of a deep mental disorder, so we are left in a very strange place where they may ask for spiritual advice but be very confused. One of the most memorable examples of this was Robert, who constantly asked to see a Chaplain because he was convinced that he was demon-possessed and wanted us to perform an exorcism. We managed him by praying with him for peace, and sought help and advice from the mental health specialists. Apparently, Robert was well known to them and was in fact suffering from the after-effects of alcohol addiction, which manifested itself in a sort of hallucination. This explained the 'dark thing' he described on his shoulder. It would have been so easy to rush in and deal with the apparent 'spiritual' problem, which was in fact a mental condition. However, I often did pray with any who asked for a blessing – everyone needs the peace of God!

Another example was Anthony, who also requested a Chaplain to come and pray with him. Initially he had been asking about forgiveness, and we visited him quite frequently and took Holy Communion to him when he requested it. Although a Roman Catholic by background, he was quite happy to take Communion from me as he thought I was a 'good' woman! But as time went on, his behaviour became increasingly bizarre and he started to write about the devil because he thought he was demon-possessed. He started to attempt self-harm and told staff he had swallowed a razor blade – but they told me he had left the plastic cover on it when he did it. However, as time went on he became increasingly unpredictable, pacing the floor or lying in the corridor. Staff thought he had actually *tried* to be mentally ill for so long that he had actually *made* himself so. He was eventually sectioned.

Early on I learned that correct regular medication could stabilise even the most unpredictable of men. However, outside of prison, their lifestyles would be so chaotic and dysfunctional that this led, directly or indirectly, to them committing crime and ending up on the inside. Paul was the first person who showed me this. I met him in CSU as an unkempt and quite scary person. He seemed very bizarre and had a habit of coming very close to you and squinting at you. I found it very difficult to understand what he was saying to me as he seemed to make incoherent noises rather than say recognisable words. In CSU, his health declined and so they transferred him to Healthcare and managed to stabilise his medication. Amazingly a new man began to emerge. He showered and shaved and seemed to be a great deal more relaxed. He reminded me of the man from the Gerasene region – 'dressed and in his right mind'. His speech was improved and I was able to exchange a few sentences with him, but he still kept on coming very close to me. One day I went into the TV room and I saw him watching it about two inches away from the screen. I asked him, 'Paul, why are you close to the TV screen?' And his reply – 'I need glasses!' – taught me another useful lesson. I had found his behaviour quite intimidating but, again, with proper medical intervention he would appear a bit more 'normal'.

Apart from prisoners suffering from severe mental disorders, there are others who also have mental health problems that minimise their ability to function effectively in a 'normal' world. There are men who are vulnerable because they have very limited intelligence or coping strategies. One suspects that often they end up in prison because they are very easily led and, once in prison, are almost always at risk of suicide or self-harm because they find themselves bullied for being 'too weak' to stand up for themselves. I remember meeting Stephen, who was aged 34 but with a mental age of ten. He had been assaulted by his padmate and was very distressed. Richard was a vulnerable prisoner who had been receiving unwelcome things under his door from other prisoners. He told me that his wife had special needs and he himself had a support worker on the outside. Coping with normal life was hard enough for these men, but in the more challenging prison environment they were often completely at a loss. Occasionally there was a vulnerable prisoner who made it through by sheer force of personality in the midst of his simplicity. Everyone loved Ben because he was usually happy and had a habit of singing very loudly – especially at Christmas. In his own little world, he lived from day to day. When he was sent back to court he had a habit of telling the judge to f*** off, so that he could return to prison. He was eventually settled into some sort of supported living – and was missed!

In addition to poor copers, there are increasing numbers of men coming to prison who have some definite mental condition or disability. Interestingly, if the disability is obvious their fellow prisoners are more likely to be sympathetic and supportive. Tim had Down's syndrome but was supported rather than bullied by his peers. Peter, with cerebral palsy which had affected his walking and one arm, was also accepted and respected by his fellow prisoners. More difficult to appreciate was Stuart, who had a brain tumour. I met him and he talked about the complex and traumatic bereavements he had suffered. He told me that his tumour had affected his behaviour – hence his prison sentence. Jonathan with Huntington's disease was on a suicide book because he felt that since his illness was incurable there was no real reason to live anyway.

With an increasingly elderly population we also see those with various stages of dementia and Alzheimer's. Trevor was one such, and found it difficult to communicate with much lucidity. I remember trying to help him remember to send out a visiting order to a relative who would visit him, and also trying to explain to him that a close relative had died, which appeared to mean very little. He stayed in Healthcare for many weeks and then they put him on a regular Unit and gave him a job assembling magnets. Here the lads with him talked to him and began to ask him about the war and he began to tell them stories about his youth, which intrigued them and certainly helped him.

Many prisoners on Induction will tell me that they are dyslexic or suffer from ADHD, which may have resulted in their early exit from the education system. I was slightly amused by some who regaled me with details of other disorders with which they had been apparently diagnosed; the most notable being ODD which stands for Oppositional Defiant Disorder, the symptoms of which are a difficulty in doing what you are told, and Explosive Personality Disorder, which manifests itself in outbursts of rage and anger. There are multitudinous personality disorders which result in individuals feeling different from the 'normal' person, and these do not necessarily require psychiatric intervention. Yet many prisoners would probably fall into this category and certainly many are aware of this – often to excuse their bad behaviour.

We also see more and more prisoners suffering from autism and Asperger's. The difficulties of managing these prisoners are illustrated by Lawrence, a very intelligent university graduate who had a degree in Physics and was studying for a Master's. He got into trouble with the law and ran away. He tried to jump off a bridge, but the police stopped him. In the struggle that ensued, one of the police officers was hit and so Lawrence was sent to prison. He presented a very low demeanour and did not communicate very much. He was reluctant to maintain his personal hygiene. At one point, I spoke to his mother who told me that Lawrence saw things as 'very black and white', symptomatic of an Asperger's sufferer. His mum also explained that Lawrence could not bear showers because the stream of water was greatly magnified to his senses. The Healthcare staff soon managed this by encouraging him to use a sink more imaginatively. To keep him occupied someone found him a physics textbook and he would spend ages reading it and writing out formulae. Because he had tried to commit suicide we had to put him on a suicide watch and ask him repeatedly through the day about his ideation of this. His mother had told me that he didn't 'do' feelings, so it was no use asking him 'how he was' as he could not comprehend this. I did try it one day and remember the look of complete puzzlement that passed over his face. I had to resort to very pragmatic conversation whilst he was poring over his formulae. 'Are you going to commit suicide today?' I asked. I received replies such as, 'I will consider the logic of suicide after court,' and, 'There is a 99.9% chance that I will commit suicide at some point.' Faced with such enigmatic responses we were forced to maintain him on a suicide watch until he finally went back to court and was released into the care of his parents.

Prison brings together a concentration of the problems of society on the outside, and the treatment of the mentally ill is one enormous concern. Prison highlights the problem; it was a place never designed to be a psychiatric establishment, and the care of mentally ill prisoners is exacting and time-consuming. In my opinion there needs to be much more support and care available in the community – not back into the vast old institutions, but maybe the return of the asylum, not for 'lunatics' but, as their name supposes, as 'a place of safety'. I would like to see communities where people with mental health difficulties could live together in a sheltered environment, hopefully being self-supporting by providing work or recycling to generate income, but to also be in a structured place where medication is dispensed and administered so that it is not neglected. I did weep sometimes at those who had ended up in prison, primarily because of their mental vulnerability. If we removed the poor copers and had a better strategy for treating those who have severe mental health issues in a more suitable environment, the prison population would be reduced significantly and there would be more time to deal with other issues that might assist rehabilitation.

Pause for reflection

Our mental health, or lack of it, has a great impact on our wellbeing. How sympathetic am I to those who suffer mental illness or disorder?
Do I pray for those who are depressed and low, and those whose own behaviour has led them into a dark place? Do I think that they are worth praying for?
How do I perceive those born with a disability that affects their behaviour?

Prayer

Lord, the mind is such a complex area and so difficult to understand, and yet You met with those who were struggling in their minds and reached out to them in love, healing and forgiveness. Lord, in our ignorance and fear of the unknown, may we be filled with Your compassion for all those who suffer in mind as well as body, and who are in need of healing. Amen.

CHAPTER 5

Little Boy Lost
The plight of young offenders

...punishing the children for the sin of the parents...

Exodus 20:5

In our prison, we receive men from the age of 18, and there is no upper age limit. Those who are aged 18 to 21 are classified as Young Offenders or, more recently, Young Adults, and are treated in a slightly different way to the older prisoners. Clearly there is a massive need to try to get these young men out of crime and the cycle of re-offending that becomes so difficult to break. We meet them along with all the other 'cons' on Induction. Sometimes they try and play 'Jack the lad' and are loud and disruptive, but more often they are quiet and what we call 'flaky', especially if this is their first time in prison. There is an interesting dynamic if we receive a lot of Young Adults at one time, as they will gravitate to each other and may well be noisier as a group. For many of them, there is the feeling of safety in numbers; aware of their vulnerability, they prefer to remain together and appear more of a force to be reckoned with. I recall an older man coming to our prison for the first time who had been in a lot of other adult jails and he confessed to be running scared of these youngsters who often appeared so wild and disrespectful.

When having conversations with these youngsters on a one-to-one basis, a completely different side of them may emerge. Often, they will share very openly with me and are quite honest about their situations. Most of them are polite and pleasant, and one is left wondering how they ever ended up in prison. And yet most of them come from fragmented and dysfunctional backgrounds, which they tend to see as 'normal' because they know nothing else. Nicholas, aged 19, came over to the chapel. His dad had died when Nicholas was 12 and he didn't know where his mother was. His grandparents had died and so had his uncles and aunts. Nicholas had no girlfriend. He used the phrase, 'You just have to get on with it, Miss,' without a shred of self-pity. Tim, again aged 19, wanted a Prison Visitor – a volunteer who would visit him once a week in the Visits Hall. His only outside contact was with his social worker. He had been in care all over the country his whole life. He found it very difficult to make appropriate relationships, hence his crime. I felt that what he had lost was any understanding of love, as he had never experienced any in the normal way of things. Some of the Young Adults, when asked about their home life, would tell me that they had been 'sofa-surfing', an expression that was new to me, but which is defined as staying temporarily with a series of friends and relatives, sleeping for example on their sofa. Worse still, when I went through the usual list of parents, girlfriend, wife, partner to see if they had any support on the outside, sadly the answer was often completely negative. Through all my years in prison, I never failed to be visibly moved at the thought that these youngsters, still in their teens, had no one on the outside who seemed to care whether they were alive or dead.

Those youngsters who *do* have families around them have often experienced almost a complete lack of parenting. Parents may have died or are absent, or the youngsters have been placed in care from a very early age. I remember one telling me he was put into care at the age of two years because he was a 'difficult child'. Chris said he had a request for me: 'How could he have a job like a Chaplain?' He then told me that his mum had died two weeks before he came into prison for the first time, but he had been estranged from her. His father was in prison too. He had a half-sister, but didn't know where she was. He was 19, had no relatives, but three A levels and was going to be put into a shelter when he left prison until he could be found a hostel. Paul was sent to us from Education as he was distressed. He told me that Mum and Dad were both heroin addicts and now Mum was dying of cancer but continued to drink and not look after herself. His comment, 'I have to be a parent to my Mum', really touched me. He was 20 years old and had fathered a baby at 15 – but the baby was the best thing in his life and all he wanted was his little family. He had three younger brothers and sisters, all cared for by Nan and Auntie, who had offered him somewhere to live when he got out. He never went to school but he knew how to get money to survive, and clothed himself from the age of ten by stealing. He knew it was wrong and didn't want to associate with those who got him into trouble. He had come to ask for prayer before he went to court. I didn't see him again after that.

On many occasions, I have wished that somehow, we could take each of these 'little boys lost' and start them over again with some decent parenting, which would not only give them love but also appropriate discipline and boundaries. It is obvious that so many crave love and attention, and they often form the most unfortunate liaisons with girls and may well produce children into the bargain. The relationships are often disastrous because they have had no role model or teaching and are still at heart children desperate for attention.

In some cases, although their parents are not at all supportive or loving, these young men still desperately long for them to be around. Mikey's mum rang and said that his grandfather had died and she would come and tell him because she thought he might be difficult. I sat with them in Visits and he was volatile but did quieten down. Mum promised to start visiting him. A few weeks later I met him after he had been put on 'Basic' for fighting – meaning he had lost certain privileges as punishment. He was clearly very wound up. When I asked if his mother had visited he said that she hadn't and that was what had made him so angry. He said that when he got out of prison he was going to ring her up and tell her he wanted nothing more to do with her. All I could see was a lost child desperate for attention. He was being very demanding and difficult, and by being this way he was very hard work for his mum. He wanted her attention, but he was in fact driving her away because his behaviour left her exhausted. The less she responded, the worse he got – a very sad, vicious cycle.

Often prisoners' family backgrounds are so unsettled and violent that any role modelling has been negative in the extreme. I was startled when a young man told me that he lived with his grandmother who 'couldn't be arsed to visit'. His girlfriend was pregnant but would have a termination if he didn't get bailed. He said that if his father didn't bring him in any clothes as instructed by his grandmother, he would 'beat him up' when he got out. Another lad, Trevor, was running scared when he arrived in prison as he said he had a very substantial amount of money 'on his head' because one of his relatives had shot someone. He wished to be transferred somewhere else where he was less likely to meet any of the rival gang's associates. He was the epitome of the major issue of gang culture. One can understand why these damaged youngsters, who have no stable background or care, readily join up with older gang leaders in their neighbourhoods, who act as role models to them. In the gangs they find acceptance and an identity in becoming part of a fraternity. Here they are cared for, given things to do and have a protection, as the gang will stand up for them. And the buzz of rival gang warfare and revenge is exciting to a degree. It seems that only when they get much older that they begin to realise that running scared is not the most satisfactory way of life.

Another common issue tends to be the youngsters' very limited educational involvement. Many of them have dropped out of school at an early age, or at least their attendance has been patchy. They seem to learn more from the 'university of life', and they sometimes speak of the way in which they had had to fend for themselves from very young. Daniel told me he was in prison for nicking a satnav in order to get 'scran' (food). He slept on the streets although he had lived with Mum in a house that was condemned and they were evicted. He didn't want to talk about his mum. He had been of no fixed abode (NFA) in several parts of the country and was really glad to be back in prison for three square meals without the need for robbing. I first encountered him because he was self-harming and he said he did this because he heard voices in his head telling him to do it. After a bike accident three months previously, the hallucinations had got worse and he had no regular means of getting medication whilst he lived on the streets.

From the moment youngsters arrive in prison, they are given opportunities to improve and further their education. Sometimes this chance may be the turning point of their lives. Ben was on a 'suicide book' when I spoke to him. As we worked through his issues we discussed what he could do in prison to make something out of his time there. I suggested that he made education a priority. As with many of these youngsters, Ben's self-confidence was very low. However, a few weeks later he came and to say thank you because I had inspired him to achieve something.

A few days after that, he came over again, proudly waving five certificates which he had just been awarded. He found that he could 'do it'.

Just occasionally we do get in young men who are educated and come from a fairly stable background. This illustrates that sometimes people do end up in prison simply because they have made very poor life choices. I think of Martin who was a university student in his first year. He had left home and started his course, but had a secret addiction which he nurtured. He was addicted to fruit machines and, very soon, instead of lectures, he was frequently visiting the local arcade. He quickly used up his loan allocation for the term and then started to borrow money from his friends. All appeared to be under control until towards the end of term, when his friends started needing their money back and there was nothing to give them. In a desperate attempt to fix his problem, Martin went into a sweet shop with a toy pistol intending to terrorise the shopkeeper into handing over some money, but instead he ended up in prison for a few years. This was hardly in his career plan, but I am sure that given the right support he would be unlikely to repeat this offence.

Some youngsters carry a huge burden of sorrow. Many have already suffered horrendous bereavements, which have led to anger as well as grief. Paul came over to chapel to light a candle for his girlfriend. She had given birth to their daughter and then committed suicide. He had also lost both grandparents, a brother in Afghanistan, a best mate from an overdose and his sister who had died in his arms as a tiny baby. He went on to say that he had been thrown out of home in his early teens by his mum's boyfriend. Yet he showed no self-pity. During all this he had gained GCSEs and set up his own painting and decorating business. He was looking forward to going back to live with an aunt when he got out.

For others, there is an immense burden of guilt for their offences and the effects they have had on others. Simon was driving a car with his girlfriend next to him when he crashed. He walked away virtually unscathed but she died. His face was so sad and he struggled with grief and guilt simultaneously. During his time in prison, his nan's health deteriorated and eventually she too died. I took the phone call from his family and sat with Simon as they gave him the news over the phone. I still remember seeing his face absolutely etched with grief – almost grey. Simon was a model prisoner and one liked by all. During his time in prison he sought every way to tackle issues in his life. The most amazing thing that he achieved was to take part in a 'marathon' by running circuits of the gym. His fellow prisoners sponsored him, and with some other lads he raised a considerable amount of money for the victims of road accidents. He has never returned to prison.

Many youngsters will resort to self-harm as a coping mechanism and often as an ingrained habit and, as we shall see later, as a means to get attention as they have no one's. One such lad told me he had put a noose round his neck 'to give the staff something to do'. Adam had actually carved into his arm with a razor blade, 'I am truly sorry for evrythink'. He had such a violent past but felt he was to blame for it because he became violent when abused by his stepfather and so was put into care along with all the other children in the family. His imprisonment had resulted from his heavy cannabis use which he had taken to try and cope with the pain. He was so wanting to change and make his life worthwhile. Away from their peers and the need to impress or to 'fit in', we often see these 'little boys lost' desperately trying to make better sense of their lives with no structure outside to support them.

In prison, we increasingly use the mentor system, where older 'cons' come alongside youngsters to encourage them into education and training and to warn them against the use of drugs and alcohol. The older cons exert a sort of 'Fletch effect', like the character in *Porridge* – they stand in as the fathers/grandfathers that these lads have never had. The older prisoners can see themselves in these youngsters, and so they are keen to help them to live in a different way before they get into the lengthy prison sentences that they themselves have received. Other prisoners will sit alongside youngsters who cannot read and write and will teach them on a one-to-one basis. The youngsters, out of public gaze and possible ridicule, often find this is the first place where they get to grips with these basic skills – they will take instruction more readily from a fellow prisoner than a trained teacher.

The sad thing is that when these youngsters leave jail they nearly always return to their original chaotic and often dysfunctional environment. It takes great strength of character and determination to begin to walk in a different direction; one that is at variance to all they have previously experienced. Often as they arrive in jail we hear the heart-felt comment, 'I need to sort out my life, Miss.' They come to talk to the Chaplains about this, not because they have any particular spiritual enquiry, but because they see us as 'people they can talk to'. One lad met me on a unit and asked, 'Miss, will you call me over to the chapel and say nice things?' This was probably in response to a previous visit when he had visited to mark a bereavement.

When we start to talk to them in the chapel, the topics of God and faith often do come up because of the surroundings. Their previous spiritual understanding and commitment is usually very limited. When lads under the age of 30 are asked what, if any, religion they follow, about 90% will respond with 'Nil'. There is a residual adherence from those who are Roman Catholics and sometimes have been taken to church as a child, often by their grandparents, but otherwise there is very little understanding. One of my colleagues once asked a lad, who was of Irish descent, 'What is your faith?' The lad misunderstood the Chaplain's local accent, understanding 'faith' as 'feet'! The astonishing answer was given: 'Size 8, Father.' Other lads will simply ask me what a religion is. Yet often in the chapel when I ask a prisoner if I may pray with him, they are more than happy. If they can read, they also enjoy our Christian storybooks, real-life testimonies of lads who are just like them. Just occasionally we do find a lad who has had some Christian background, although sometimes their ideas are a little confused and confusing. Anthony wanted a Bible, although he also came over to discuss whether it was right to earn money by minding cannabis plants for 'a friend'. In further encounters when we had talked about forgiveness, he asked if he could pray for forgiveness and with great fervour prayed that God would 'let his dog know that he was forgiven for biting Nan'. But in between it all there was some spiritual awareness and, just before he left, Anthony presented me with picture of John the Baptist and made the comment that God had come into his life, but he knew that he had to help himself.

It is so difficult to see how we can make life better for these young men and somehow work with the wreckage of their lives to that point. Whilst one must never accept behaviour and acts that hurt and damage others, it is easy to see how these men have ended up where they are and, whilst their decisions and actions are their own, their conditioning and upbringing have so affected their understanding of right and wrong that without some sort of complete metamorphosis, it is not surprising that once they have been to prison the first time, they are quite likely to come back again – and again. If, at the age of nine, your dad disappears and you are the eldest child in the family, Mum comes to you and says, 'You're the man of the family now. You have got to provide for us.' She sends you out shoplifting, so what moral code do you learn? How can it be wrong if your parent tells you to do it – and surely providing for your family is good? This happened to a young man whose brothers also intermittently came to prison for the same reason. The middle brother really did want to live life in a Christian way, as his mother professed to be a believer. We had many conversations and I challenged him about his lifestyle and he admitted that over the course of time shoplifting had actually become an addiction and he found it difficult to give it up because of the 'buzz' he got from it. What can break the ingrained habits and standards? Surely it is only the grace of God changing these lads from the inside out and bringing healing to the broken places, that they may stand any chance of breaking free, not just from crime and prison, but to become the young men they were really meant to be.

Pause for reflection

What impact do we have on youngsters in our family, and in the wider world? Do our attitudes to them help them, or are we more anxious to criticise and compare them to the way we were when we were their age?
Do we pray for our fractured society and the young people who are growing up in it? Can we see ways of reaching out and helping youngsters develop more healthy attitudes and activities?

Prayer

Father, we cry out to You for the youth of today, surrounded as they are by so many pressures and fears. Lord, as we see the brokenness in our society, we also see a generation that often wants to live without You. Lord, we pray that You would help us to know how we can be part of bringing healing to this damaged world – which is a massive undertaking! Lord, above all we pray that youngsters may be able to come and know the healing grace and love that only You can bring to their lives. Amen.

CHAPTER 6

Crying Out for Help

The problems underlying self-harm and suicide

[Disclaimer: This chapter is not for the squeamish!]

> So they shouted louder and slashed themselves with swords and spears, as was their custom, until their blood flowed
>
> 1 Kings 18:28

I remember vividly when I witnessed it for the first time: a man deliberately cutting himself to draw blood. He had just arrived in prison and had a razor blade secreted on his person, and it is not permitted to remove this forcibly. I came to have an Induction conversation with him and, as I began to speak, he sliced his arm and was collecting the blood in a cardboard urine container. I am not very good with blood, and began to feel nauseous, but manfully tried to carry on. Each question I asked led to another cut and, in the end, I felt so ill that I terminated the conversation and escaped into the office. The Healthcare staff were understanding and told me I had done the right thing – as soon as I had gone away, the prisoner had stopped cutting himself and only resumed when he had an audience.

Ideation of suicide and self-harm (SASH) is extremely common and rising among the prison population. Clearly, with the number of suicide attempts and actual suicides that are now seen in prison, every comment or indication that a prisoner makes regarding taking his own life is treated very seriously. Whilst

some prisoners will intentionally try and take their lives, many others engage in
the act of self-harm, which in some cases can result in death. If a prisoner inflicts
any physical harm to himself, however trivial, or states his intention of so doing,
he is placed on an Assessment, Care in Custody and Teamwork book (ACCT
book). This document ensures that from the first declaration of the prisoner of his
intent, he is immediately 'watched' at regular intervals to make sure of his state,
and spoken to at frequent intervals. As soon as possible an Assessor sits with him
and asks a set of questions about why he feels like he does and whether this is a
pattern of behaviour or a 'one off.' We also work with the prisoner to produce
a Care Plan, with some clear strategy to help him through this time. Chaplains
are required to see every prisoner who is put onto an ACCT book on the first
day that it is opened, and to visit them at least once a week. This is an increasingly time-consuming activity for Chaplaincy, as at any one time there may be
30 prisoners on such a book. During the course of a year this really adds up. In
one year alone, Chaplaincy had visited over 1,000 such prisoners. A colleague
and myself were also trained Assessors and, with other pressures, are called upon
very frequently as our time is relatively flexible. In that same year, this colleague
and I conducted over 20 per cent of all the Assessments. Whilst there is a fixed
protocol to follow, I often found that these Assessments provided a 'way in' with
the lads because during the course of the interview we unearthed issues that we
could later follow up. Some of the prisoners who did not want to speak to Officers
would actually be more open with us as we were seen to be 'non-judgmental'.

In the last few years, we have seen a shift in the reasons prisoners give as to why
they have been put on an ACCT book. In the past it was predominately because
they had strong feelings of wishing to end their lives, but now most speak of self-
harm rather than suicide. The reasons for self-harm are becoming increasingly
diverse and complex. Unfortunately, a large number of those who self-harm are
attempting to manipulate in some way. Because we cannot ignore even the tiniest
scratch in case it is evidence of intent to commit suicide, they harm themselves
in order to have a forum with a Manager and attract attention for some reason.
When asked the reason for the self-harm, we receive responses such as, 'I did it
to get meds' or, 'I've got no tobacco' or, 'I need to phone my girlfriend'… 'I need
to speak to the Director'. Sometimes they will simply confess, 'I did it for effect'
or 'for something to do'. Whilst apparently time-wasting, they cannot be ignored

because sometimes there is a need which they cannot articulate. Often, when I probed, I would discover other issues, such as bereavement, which they had been reluctant to mention until they felt more at ease with me. Often the issues that had led them to self-harm were not those that could be easily dealt with, such as wanting to be at the scan of their baby, or even to get out of jail! Many men who end up in prison are not good at coping with life in general and, like children, will sometimes 'cry wolf' to get what they think they need – as soon as they need it! It takes great skill and professionalism from the staff to help these men. Sensitivity and yet firmness and fairness are needed to help them build coping strategies to deal with the petty annoyances of life in general. Sometimes the methods of self-harm they use are as bizarre as their reasons. I vividly remember being told that one lad, whilst in CSU had attempted to take his own life by eating plastic knives and forks. To make it more palatable, he had sandwiched them between slices of bread and butter! Fortunately, his attempt was unsuccessful.

Early on in my time as a Chaplain, I used my experience as a teacher to suggest that keeping occupied was often a good thing. Activity helped people to cope so that they were not just sitting in their cells feeling miserable. I handed out endless wordsearches (which even those who cannot read can often attempt), sudoku puzzles and colouring pictures. The original pictures I used were in fact outlines from *The Book of Kells*, which represents the four Gospels, but which prisoners saw as like tattoo art outlines! In later years, I extended my portfolio for them and gave them pictures they could colour and send to their children or girlfriends, which gave them an added incentive to complete them. Interestingly, we were using the therapy of colouring long before it gained the prestige it has today! Christian books at this time were also given and generally well accepted because reading them gave the men something constructive to do.

The more serious self-harmers were often those who had developed a habit of doing it and almost become addicted to it as a means of coping. The more often they did it, the more likely they were to continue in that way. Psychologists will say that their reason might have been to do with using pain as a means of 'feeling alive' or of channelling emotional pain into physical pain. Certainly, many spoke to me of the way it made them feel they were in control.

Often the reason for self-harm may appear fairly trivial. When I asked Michael what his problems were, he replied, 'The world is broken.' He had become stressed by watching news on the TV of children suffering. He had been in care and had looked after himself since the age of 13. He had little contact with his mum and was in for a charge against his girlfriend. Many of these men are deeply depressed and actually with just cause. Life has not been very kind to them, nor has it ever been easy. Adding to that the complexity of human relationships with other people who are also damaged, it is easy to see how the weight of this sometimes becomes intolerable. As a reason for self-harm, men will tell me they did it to 'annoy their girlfriend' or 'to make my wife suffer'. One even told me that he started to self-harm when his baby cried and it was his turn to get up and feed him!

Self-harmers are often very complex people and the solution to their habit is not always straightforward. Alex was a prolific self-harmer who had had many prison sentences. He had cut his arms so much that they were now in a state where the doctor said that if he continued to harm himself in this way, he could no longer stitch the flesh together because it was so damaged. If he continued in this way, he would lose his arm entirely. Alex was a highly intelligent and creative man and was seen by psychiatrists and counsellors and mental health doctors, but nothing seemed to work. In the end, they sent him to a secure mental health hospital and when he came back he had stopped self-harming. We were all amazed and I asked him what had happened. He said that 'If you stay in prison, you will get to the end of your sentence, but if you are in a mental hospital you might stay there for ever.' Something had obviously got through to him. He also said to me, 'Katy, every day of my life I feel like self-harming, but then I pick up my guitar and sing.' He had discovered displacement therapy! Because of his meteoric change, he was allowed to address the whole staff about self-harm and told us that he had been harming himself from the age of 11 when he witnessed his father raping his mother. Interestingly, through all my encounters with Alex, we often did speak of God and he always said that he did know Him. He told me the story of when he had been in another prison and had had a cell which overlooked a flat roof and it was his custom to throw out his toast crumbs to the birds that congregated there. One day there was a bird with a broken leg and he tried very hard to make sure that this poor bird got his toast crumbs, but the bird kept hopping away. He said he felt God say to him, 'You're just like that bird;

everyone is trying to help you and you just keep turning away.' Alex did manage to stay out of prison several years after that but, unfortunately, has returned after a tragedy in his personal life sent him back down his 'old path'.

When, as an Assessor, I asked the question, 'What positive things do you have in your life that might prevent you from harming yourself?', I was often deeply saddened and humbled when they replied, 'Nothing, Miss.' Listening to their stories I could see why. Philip, a 'frequent flier' came back into prison having been out only five days, and sleeping in a cave. Because he had had no methadone he felt there was nothing left to live for. He was always a deeply depressed man and really did have no one on the outside and found it very difficult to make anything out of life. Years ago, he had been tattooed all over his face and I used to find him quite scary but, as I got to know him I saw a very deeply sad man who actually asked if 'God would make him better'. Liam had just received a very lengthy prison sentence for a horrendous crime he had committed when high on drink and drugs. His partner had recently died from cystic fibrosis and he was not allowed contact with any family member because of the circumstances of the crime. How did he make sense of life?

From a Christian point of view, it was interesting that on several occasions the reason men gave for self-harm was to do with guilt, and this will be explored in a later chapter. For example, Paul, a first-timer in prison claimed he was in for 'fraud' but actually it was a sex offence. He spoke of wanting to kill himself because he was ashamed (and also running scared about being in prison). Even more poignant was Howard, again with a lengthy sentence but so anxious about his mum who had rung in to us and was so tearful and worried. He seemed to have a more stable background than some, and I guessed he was easily led. He made the statement, 'I wish I'd never been born, because I've caused so much trouble.' He wished his own life to cease because in his view it would be better if he wasn't here.

As we speak to these lads, we encourage them to engage with the prison system. We are never going to solve all their problems or take away all their anxieties, but we work to try and support them when they need it most and to get them any help that may alleviate deep-seated problems.

For many, they are on a 'suicide book' for only a matter of days or a few weeks, but there are chronic sufferers whose mental state makes it extremely difficult to be sure that they will not spontaneously do something that will damage their health. Those who suffer several mental conditions, such as schizophrenia, tell of hearing 'voices' that tell them to self-harm. Sometimes the 'voices' will tell them to harm others and so they would rather hurt themselves than inflict injury on another. They often self-harm in strange ways, like Colin who had cut out all the eyes on his tattoos with a razor blade. Bizarre behaviour may also be due to the latest phenomenon that is sweeping our prisons which concerns NPSs (new psychoactive substances), which used to be called 'legal highs'. A variety of compounds are found in these substances which are readily available in products such as fish fertiliser. They are known colloquially by many names: Mamba, Spice, Clockwork Orange, and their effects are unpredictable and extremely serious. Even a small dose can precipitate a massive reaction and the outcome depends on the individual and what they have taken. I remember one of the first men I visited who had been put on a suicide book because he had taken Mamba. He told me he felt as though 'death was coming for him', and was almost terrified to death because of this. On the whole, these effects are short-lived, but as the sensation is so real and vivid at the time, men are at risk of seriously harming themselves whilst under the influence.

With such a rigorous support system in place in prison, suicide itself is thankfully not that frequent, especially if compared to the percentage in the population in general. However, cases are rising and every death is a tragedy. Chaplains are often sent out alongside a Family Liaison Officer (FLO) to be the people who break this horrendous news to the families concerned. This has to be one of the hardest tasks ever assigned. We are sent to the next of kin, although even that is somewhat problematic in itself in view of the dysfunctional backgrounds of many prisoners. Sometimes we need a police escort just to enter the neighbourhood of their kin. Once there we have to enter their world and break this devastating news. More often than not it is accepted stoically by the relatives and they are seldom that surprised. Just occasionally suicide is undertaken by a lad from a 'good' background and the devastation it causes is unspeakable. We were sent to a very ordinary couple to break the ultimate bad news and they were so shocked that we were asked to leave the house. In the midst of the FLO explaining the procedures I was struggling to try and give just some crumb of support to these broken parents, as I had known this lad and he had attended chapel from time to time. As we hurriedly took our leave, all I could think to say was, 'I knew Howard and he was a lovely lad.' Then we were ushered out of the door. The next day the father rang up to apologise for their hostile behaviour and mentioned that his wife had been touched by those very few words. Nothing can ever reach to exactly where people are except the love and grace of God.

Bereaved families are invited into prison if they so wish, to see the cell where their loved one died and to speak to staff. We offer a memorial service for anyone who has died whilst in prison, and this takes the same format whether it is for a prisoner who has died of natural causes or through suicide, or for a member of staff known to us all. These can be deeply moving occasions. If the prisoner had been with us for a while, sometimes their fellow inmates will come out to the front and speak of them, and one realises that prison is very much a supportive community in many respects, and for many of them their life centres around fellow prisoners rather than people on the outside. Early on in my time in prison, a lad took his own life the night after he had come to prison. This was not his first time inside, and when we looked up his next of kin, he had written the name of our prison, even though he did have relatives on the outside. When I went to speak to other lads on his Unit to check they were OK, as an incident like this shakes many other people, they said to me, 'He came to die amongst his friends, Miss. On the outside he lived as a drug addict in a burned-out car, and if he had died out there, no one would have known who he was – but in here we all knew him.' At his memorial service, a traveller who had received no formal education, but who had taught himself to read and write, read out the most moving poem for him, which he had written himself.

It is at these times that we can reach out gently as Chaplains, in a way that is unique to us. I went with a bereaved family to the mortuary as they went to say goodbye to their very young son. I felt deeply that I needed to do something to give them God's comfort, but wasn't sure if they had any religious inclination. Just as we were about to go in to see the son, I gave to the mum one of our wooden crosses which we give to lads when they come to chapel after a bereavement, and I asked her if she would like to have it. Without hesitation, she accepted it and all the time we were looking on this beautiful but lifeless young man's face, she held the cross close to her. When I asked if I could pray, the whole family were willing. A few weeks later, several family members came into the chapel for the lad's memorial service and I stood at the door to greet them. The mother immediately came to me and said, 'Can all my family members have crosses too?' Such an inconsequential object in itself, made of cheap balsa, yet signifying so much. Words in themselves can rarely reach the deepest places but, sometimes, just to hold on to the cross in the darkest times is all we can do.

Pause for reflection

What coping mechanisms do we use in our daily life? How can we cultivate trust in God in all things?

How do we pray and reach out to those for whom coping is much more difficult?

How can we share the hope that is within us in a way that is practical and relevant?

Prayer

Father, we cry out to You for those who struggle with life and who feel there is no hope and no reason to live. We pray for those who stand alongside people in distress and pray that You would endue them with Your wisdom and strength, that they might give the support and care that so many need. Lord, above all, we pray that those who struggle in the darkest despair may find Your healing touch of forgiveness and restoration as You bring wholeness to their brokenness and despair. Amen.

CHAPTER 7

A Tangled Web

The dysfunctional nature of family life and its effects

The heart is deceitful above all things and beyond cure. Who can understand it?

Jeremiah 17:9

'Every Prisoner is Someone's Son.' This was my title for a talk at a Christian gathering for mothers. It was a reminder that everyone starts their lives in the same way, but not all have the same opportunities for growth. For many of us who have experienced love, security and good parenting, it is very difficult to appreciate how hard it is for someone who has not experienced those things. Each child is born as the result of an act of love or lust, prepared for or spontaneous, wanted or from an act of drunken violence. From then onwards the path may be smooth and constructive or hard and violent, and any mixture in between. Our childhood experience of nurture (or our lack of it) and our own nature will affect who we become. Many of us have been brought up with an understanding of right and wrong which aligns with that of wider society. For those with different moral codes, 'right and wrong' may differ from our interpretation.

I found it difficult not to be shocked sometimes by the stories that prisoners related to me their childhoods. Kevin was given skunk at 18 months old and his sister was fed with Ecstasy tablets and hit by her father, so that she became mentally ill. Both children were put into foster care. Kevin told me that he felt guilty for letting his foster parents down by ending up in prison, and wanted to get his life sorted out. He was dyslexic and had Irlen syndrome, which had hampered his progress in school. As is often the case, there was no hint of self-pity, although he did add that he hadn't been able to cry since he was five years old. George came to the chapel to light a candle for the funeral of a friend of his father, who had brought him up after George had gone off the rails at 14 and got thrown out by his dad. His mother was an alcoholic and had stabbed him when he was 11 years old, and Granddad had 'played with him' from the age of four. He went on to say that at Christmas they never had any presents and one year he saved up his own money to buy himself a new 'trackie' for Christmas Day. He had such a sad face.

Children often not only live with uncertainty, but also witness terrible things happening around them. From an early age the only language that seems to count is violence, and it is not surprising that as these children grow up they resort to violence also. Wayne got involved in a bad fight in prison. I spoke to his auntie who said that he came from a large family and had been a 'difficult child'. He and his brother had been locked up by their parents because they were so bad and consequently he had been put into care, but when the family circumstances were examined, all of his brothers and sisters were also removed from their parents, who then blamed Wayne for breaking up the family. His crime was stabbing his own brother. I met a very timid young man who said his auntie had told him to 'do what he was told to do'!

Kieran broke down in tears. He and his mother had been in a refuge since he was two years old to escape from his father. Kieran's greatest fear was that he would become like his father. He was in prison for hitting his girlfriend when she had cut up his clothes. His brother had been murdered five years before. He was so aware of his own problems with anger, which were fuelled by alcohol. Will was a bouncer who said he had found he had a heart – he didn't want to be violent anymore. He told me that his mother made him wear his brother's old shoes which were too small for him. Will told her that if he didn't get new shoes he would go out robbing. As I listened to Will, he kept mentioning that he had sent people round to deal with people, telling them to 'give them a slap – not a real fight'. In his view this constituted a move in the right direction!

As the years go by, children become men, and their exposure to violence becomes even more pronounced. The sheer awfulness of some of the incidents they have witnessed is difficult to describe. When I told Francis of the shooting of his cousin, he didn't seem to be at all surprised; Francis himself had been attacked with a machete. Hughie freely admitted that his life had fallen to bits through drugs and alcohol and because of his anger. He had been abused as a child and seen violence, so he 'learned violence'. He was alleged to have hit his girlfriend, although he denied it. But he also told me that he had started to pray and did believe in God – and knew he needed help.

As one considers the background of many of those who come to prison, and the ways of processing that they have already learned – and even the survival techniques they have already had to employ – it is not surprising that truth and fantasy can be easily interchanged. The trouble is that for many of these men, the way of honesty and truth as we might understand, it is not the way they see the world or cope with it. Some of their stories were distressing and there was no doubt in my mind that many of them were true but, from time to time, one would also hear stories that had been embellished – perhaps just to gain the sympathy vote. One has to be aware that honesty is not always the go-to reaction of these young men, who may have had to had to get through life by living on their wits. The line between truth and lie may be blurred for many of them.

I remember taking time with Robert, a chronic alcoholic, who told me that he had lost both his uncle and his granddad at the same time. Whilst at their funeral, Robert's father had been murdered with a pickaxe, his mum had died and his sister had committed suicide. Robert had been in touch with a church and, when I rang to speak to the pastor, I got a different version: 'Robert lies!' Robert had also told me that he had self-harmed a few days before, and had been hospitalised before coming into prison. The pastor said the truth was that Robert had had an epileptic fit when he was sleeping rough. He had been evicted because of his alcoholic friends, and his 'self-harm' was actually scratching himself with a drawing pin!

Truth may be stranger than fiction sometimes, but in the parallel world which is unknown to most of us, the need to get through and survive may mean that the truth may not always be the first priority. And the perception of reality may be somewhat blurred. Our calling as Chaplains is to listen; to sit where they sit and allow them to tell us what they will. What we make of what they say is up to us, and I felt that even if what they told me was not 'the truth, the whole truth and nothing but the truth', they were still there as people in desperate need, who needed to find the healing of God's love in the deepest and darkest places in their lives.

One thing I did struggle with as far as deception was concerned, in prison terms is known as 'blagging'. It is the deliberate manipulation of truth in order to gain something. Very early on in my time in prison I was completely taken in by one young man. He told me that as he was being sentenced in court, a policeman came and told him that his girlfriend had committed suicide. He wanted to know when the funeral would be so that he could attend it. On the surface this seemed a completely reasonable request, and so I spent about three hours ringing around hospitals, police stations, morgues and coroners' courts to try and gain the information he required. I was unsuccessful and, when I returned to speak to the young man, I was most apologetic. He didn't seem very surprised, and the staff later told me that he had confessed he had made it up because he wanted to get a phone call to speak to the girlfriend! I remember thinking that graciousness is very hard at such times, as I had spent so long on a fruitless search. Even worse was a lad who told me that his girlfriend was in hospital and gave me the ward telephone number to ring. I was suspicious when I saw that it was a mobile number and, when I rang it, was not convinced that the recipient of the call was a member of the medical profession. I was right – it turned out to be the girlfriend herself whose contact he had recorded as a medical number. Probably this was because there was some sort of restraining order between them and normal methods of communication would not have been permitted.

In my naivety, I discovered that this practice was common not just among prisoners, but was also increasingly happening among the families of the prisoners, who would ring in with fictitious information. Every case had to be treated with respect, and in the belief that the information we were being given was true, but it often took hours to confirm a death or illness. Given the dysfunctional nature of many of their families, getting correct information from them in the first place was difficult. After several phone calls to various hospitals to locate a seriously ill relative who appeared to be nowhere, I re-rang the original informant who then proceeded to give me a completely different name that she might have been called and finally located her. But far worse were people who rang in, often at night, to tell us that a member of the prisoner's family had been in an accident or was dying. Sometimes an aggrieved girlfriend who wanted to 'punish' her erstwhile partner would give us shocking news such as a road accident involving a child. Emotions high, we would ring around frantically to find out more only to discover that the information was completely fictitious. They expected us to tell the prisoner without any checks and in the hope that, in our compassion, he would be given a phone call at this distressing time. On one occasion, the officers suspected that it was other prisoners who had conveyed the information to us because the lad involved owed them money. 'Oh, what a tangled web we weave…'

Other prisoners would make up fictitious bereavements and tell us they needed to come to the chapel to light a candle. This was a hard one because sometimes the lads find it difficult to tell anyone why they want to speak to someone, and it is socially acceptable in prisoner's eyes to go to the chapel on an anniversary or at the time of a funeral. Once with us they may well tell us the real reason for them seeking us out. I am sure that I have lit many candles for fictitious people, but I am equally sure that God sees their true motivation and understands!

One of the most bizarre deceptions I encountered was not to do with death but with marriage. In our prison, we offered a civil ceremony in part of the Administration area. This was a very low-key affair, but has to go through several stages involving registrars from the outside. A man who I shall call Sean asked to speak to me concerning marriage – a relatively commonplace procedure. He was very honest and said he had been married before and he was just waiting for his decree absolute to come through so that he could go ahead. The papers did turn up in due course (to my slight surprise), but they were not in Sean's name but in another's name. When I queried him about this he explained that his real name was the one on the divorce papers, but when in prison he always used the name of Sean and a very common surname. Suspicions were aroused and I went to check on his data. To my amazement, I found that he had at least 30 different aliases, several different dates of birth and other spellings of his current name! Who was he really? I rang Outside Probation to try and get some assistance, but the plot thickened further when they said that they would recommend we do a DNA test to discover his true identity as they also were not sure! They added to that he had a brother-in-law called by several of the same names who had an identical date of birth to him! This was the only occasion when the Director failed to give his consent to the marriage taking place in prison, as the person we had in our care could not be proved to be the same man mentioned on the divorce papers. He was transferred to another prison soon after that and a few months later I received a phone call from the Chaplaincy asking me what I knew of Sean, as he had asked them if he could get married! Needless to say, I filled them in with all that I knew.

As I write of the tangled webs woven by prisoners and their families, it would be remiss not to mention the very frayed and difficult relationships that are formed by prisoners with both their parents and any subsequent partners of the parents. Violence breeds violence, and it was not difficult to see why, if treated with indifference, neglect or abuse from an early age, and forever witnessing violence in the home, many of these lads grow up repeating the pattern. I feel that many of the men long to find unconditional love, and seek solace with their multiple partners who often have come from similar dysfunctional backgrounds and have their own problems. Certainly, many of the men seem to want to control their partners, and I was forever suggesting that they gave them a bit of 'space', that 'loving them to bits' was all very well but sometimes if you squeeze a person too hard, they cannot breathe! I think many of them looked for a mother's love (and a father's) in these relationships, and the girls could not meet those unrealistic expectations. Children seemed to be conceived readily – one man who returned to prison after being out for a week, proudly told me later that he had got three girls pregnant whilst he had been out of jail. On the whole the men seemed to really love these offspring, perhaps gaining for the first time a glimpse of someone giving them love unconditionally. Often, they were quite happy to 'bin' the girlfriend, but got very angry and aggressive if they were denied access to the children. Girls too often appeared to be quite devious – I spoke to many men who had responded to a text or phone call from their ex-partners inviting them to visit the children and when they came to the house (thereby breaking a restraining order) the girl immediately 'shopped' them to the police. This could happen time and time again and, when I suggested that they might be better off breaking away from the relationship, they did not seem able to do so as it was the only life they had known where there was some vestige of 'love'. Others also admitted that they themselves had been victims of abuse by their girlfriends and had finally retaliated.

Often, as they had nothing to draw on in terms of a parenting example, their methods of dealing with their own children were rough and ready. I remember talking to Brian, who spent all day graffitiing the names of all his children on pieces of paper, but was actually in for child cruelty. Matthew said he was a long-distance lorry driver and worked extremely hard to earn money for the family, but when he arrived home exhausted he found his partner expected him to do all the child care too because she couldn't cope. He (and she) had been convicted of child neglect. Many of the fractured relationships arose because of bad behaviour of both parents, and we often had to counsel men who had received phone calls form their girlfriends who had been told that if they wished to keep their children, they must stop seeing the father. Once off drink and drugs, these men appeared quite loving and stable, and one felt that if they could stay sober there might be a chance for some sort of restored relationship with their children at least. However, the saying 'once an addict, always an addict' is true to a large degree, and when released from prison, the temptation is obvious, whilst children need to be protected and not just left to the vagaries of the hope that someone has changed completely. I do believe that unless there is a complete heart as well as head change (by the grace of God), it is a very difficult road which is not very well supported once they leave jail.

One of the most emotional bereavements that these men may encounter in prison is that their children are adopted whilst they are in prison, meaning they lose forever those whom they love. Since this news is received when they are not high on drink or drugs, the pain is enormous. I still have a letter that a man wrote for his son who was about to be adopted, that he wished to show him when he would finally be allowed to see him again – probably in many years' time. It is such an honest piece speaking of the depths of despair at losing his only child. It was obvious that it was in the child's best interests that he should be removed from an environment where one or both parents were constantly 'out of it', but one could see also the effect this has the parents. Sometimes it is the absolute driving force that makes a man come to his senses and turn his life right around, but sadly this is often just too difficult.

As Chaplains, we often receive phone calls from the relatives of those in prison, which can be very distressing. Many a time I have had to counsel a mother who was weeping at the other end of the line. Some ring because they are worried about their son or partner, but others ring up to 'confess' to us that they cannot cope any longer with their wayward relative. This is especially true with mothers and grandmothers. On several occasions, I could tell that the person ringing was of faith or attended church or chapel and felt very guilty for their feelings. How do you carry on caring for and forgiving your son or grandson when he steals from you to buy drugs and lies about everything? The trouble with those who take drugs is that their perception of other people's needs and feelings becomes completely obliterated in the desperate need to satisfy their craving. In the cold light of detoxing, many of them realise this and the tears they shed thinking about if Nan or Granddad die whilst they are in prison, are often broken and remorseful although it is too late. But at the heart of any mother there is still an invisible, 'umbilical' tie, and those who call us often long to re-establish relationships. Kevin's mum said to me that she just wanted 'the old Kevin back, without the drugs'. They had not spoken for years, but after a family bereavement had spoken again. Interestingly, the prisoners often feel so much guilt in the light of day about the way they have treated their nearest and dearest, that they fail to keep in touch with them and even push away any attempt of reconciliation. There has to be a much a deeper work than merely saying sorry. When the men actually take time to think and are away from everyone except themselves, many of them do realise that they need to change. As Paul commented, 'Mum can't take any more.' They often form positive resolutions and actually recognise their weaknesses, but it is the carrying through of good intent that is often the stumbling block. Undoing years of harmful attitudes which have been developed through the circumstances to which they will return is no light matter. As we seek to rehabilitate prisoners it is not just a case of telling them to behave 'like us', because we have 'normal' values and expectations, but seeking to support them as they have to make a seismic shift of the way that they have always thought about life and managed themselves. We will re-examine this in a later chapter.

Pause for reflection

How has our background affected our understanding of faith?

How can we help people whose lives have been full of violence and negative influences?

How do we share the gospel of grace and love in a way that is understandable to those who have lived through difficult beginnings?

Have we found healing for our own emotional hurts, that affect and damage so much of our own thinking and spiritual development?

Prayer

Father God, we pray for those who have experienced little love and guidance from their parents. We cry out to You for those whose lives are full of fear and violence and who have absorbed the negativity and hopelessness of their environment. Father, only You can bring true healing of body, mind and spirit, and fill up the deep and damaged places with the balm of Your forgiveness and love. We pray that You would teach us to share this hope with those who so desperately need to find a better way of living. Amen.

CHAPTER 8

The Depths of Darkness:
Does God Love Paedophiles?

Discussing the hardest things to understand
from a Christian viewpoint

> He reveals the deep things of darkness and brings utter darkness
> into the light.
>
> Job 12:22

I once spoke at a ladies group, sharing some of the stories of damaged and broken lives that I have related in this book. At the end of my talk, one of the ladies asked me, 'But what about the *real* criminals?' At the time, I was a little put out, thinking she had missed my whole point, that 'criminals' are human beings, just like the rest of us. On reflection, I had to concede that many of the prisoners we dealt with were what we would term 'scallies' – those who are in for very short periods of time for crimes of shop-lifting, stealing, traffic offences and so on – and these lads are a far cry from those who cold-heartedly perform premeditated acts of serious violence.

As the prison population has increased, and it is more obvious that some prisoners are 'churned' around 'the estate' (prisons in England and Wales), we are now dealing with much more mixed populations. Local remand prisons may now receive long-term, 'heavy-duty' prisoners from elsewhere. These prisoners have very different needs to those of short-term, local offenders. I believe that some of the unrest in prison can be attributable to this newer phenomenon. It is very difficult to tailor courses, training, rehabilitation and management to such diverse needs. The requirements are completely different for a mature man midway through a 27-year sentence than for a local youngster who will only be in prison for three months. Adding to this, we are also seeing an increasing number of sex offenders coming through, being charged on historical offences, and also the massive rise in convictions for the downloading of illegal material from the internet and connected abuses. When prisoners are received into our custody, there is no 'sifting' into types, apart from separating out those who are considered to be at risk from other prisoners (Vulnerable Prisoners), usually because of the nature of their offence. This means that a 'first-timer', often 'flaky', but also very often open to reform and release, may be housed next to someone who has been in prison for a very long time, and is well acquainted with every method of manipulation and 'survival' technique, and whose release date is so distant as to be almost irrelevant.

So, from time to time we do meet some extremely dangerous and violent men who have committed terrible acts of crime. How do we cope with them as Chaplains, trying to reconcile what appears to be 'pure evil' with our ministry of non-judgmental support? This is something of an ongoing struggle for us, not only in pastoral terms, but also trying to grapple with the theology of these situations.

I have met quite a few murderers in my time, and have come to recognise why the American system recognises 'degrees' of this crime. Most of the murderers I have met have been those who have acted on the spur of the moment – 'my moment of madness', as one described it to me – when anger, often fuelled by drink or drugs, has erupted into savagery. Others have gone out with intention to injure rather than kill, but it all went terribly wrong. Still others have killed almost completely by accident. I can think of a few examples of this: a diminutive young man out for a drink with his girlfriend who threw a single punch at a lad who looked sideways at the girlfriend. The victim was felled by the blow, hit the pavement kerb and died. Two other young men had been out for a good time and, whilst driving home, saw a wheelie bin outside a house and thought it would be fun to set fire to it, which they did. It was placed beside an outhouse and, unbeknown to them, a 'man of the road' was asleep inside it. He was burned alive. Another man, who had never even had a parking ticket in his life, was driving a lorry down a motorway and, changing the music on his radio, swerved to avoid an AA man who was standing by a broken-down car. He hit the car and the driver of the vehicle was killed. The culprit was in a state of suspended shock for about three months after he arrived in prison. Whilst never condoning any act of violence, one can feel a sense of compassion for these men whose lives were forever changed in the blink of an eye.

However, occasionally one will meet those who have gone out with the express intention to injure and kill, and these are very different. There are some on the psychopathic scale who may appear outwardly to be reasonably 'normal', but on further examination have a very skewed understanding of the truth. Somehow, in their minds, the truth is not believable but the lie is.

One such man completely denied his part in the murder he had committed. He was an older man and appeared very morally upright. But the truth prevailed and, although we received phone calls from concerned Christian friends on the outside who could also not believe the allegations, he was found guilty and given more than 20 years to serve. The only time I ever saw him express any emotion was the morning after this sentence when I went to see him and asked him how his wife had taken the news. At this point he broke down and cried, but later continued to assert his innocence.

The Bible does have quite a bit to say about the awfulness of murder, but it is interesting to note that about two-thirds of the Bible was written by murderers. Moses killed on the 'spur of the moment', but King David had a definite plan and even got someone else to carry out the deed for him. St Paul, before his conversion, also planned and ensured the murders of Christians. And yet these were all mighty men of God who were used by Him in spite of what they had done. Whilst the crimes I heard about were horrendous in the extreme, I could sense the compassion of God for the men who had committed these terrible acts. As we shall see later, many of them did try to change their lives in future, as well as seek to make atonement for their wrongs.

Perhaps one of the most contentious subjects is that of sex offence and in particular paedophilia. It is very hard indeed to separate one's own feelings about such crimes committed and one's responsibility as a Christian minister. I expected to be frightened of such men but in fact many of them are almost shockingly 'normal' in demeanour. As with murder, there are degrees of this crime but, overall, the number of men convicted of these crimes is rising dramatically, due in part to the nature of material available on the internet.

Many men are in for downloading illegal images – a crime that would not have even been possible just over a decade ago. It seems to be very easy to slip into this world, and the behaviour can rapidly turn into an addiction. I think of Peter, who had Asperger's, and was a bit of a loner. He enjoyed music, which he started to download. As he did this, he 'stumbled' into images which were the beginning of his downfall. We cannot underestimate the seriousness of this in terms of abuse, but perhaps the justice system needs to find alternative methods of assisting and rehabilitating individuals like Peter in a more specialised system than prison. Specialised courses for sex offenders are available in some prisons, but there is a massive gap between supply and demand.

When speaking to such men, two things do become clear: firstly, they are apparently unaware of 'normal' boundaries and, secondly, they usually try to justify their actions. In an attempt to understand how they can commit such crimes, I can only come to the conclusion that the way they are 'wired' to think is somehow distorted. The way they perceive things is not 'normal', but it is to them. In my view, they are diseased; just as with a physical illness the body is altered, so with their 'disease' the mind is affected and leads to consequent actions. With this view, I can perceive them as fellow human beings, but with a very 'odd' way of seeing things. It is not easy and is particularly complex at times when we have to give them bad news. Often, they appear to be very moved, yet it is in a rather 'twisted' way, and it is difficult to be non-judgmental.

In the world of the prison the prevailing moral code among prisoners is in nature extremely dogmatic and hard-line. People who 'do' things to children or old ladies are completely contemptible and deserving of verbal abuse and physical punishment. 'Normal' prisoners label these men as nonces (not of normal criminal element). If there is even a vague suspicion that a fellow inmate is such a person, his life often becomes intolerable as the 'bush telegraph' – a rapid informal network of gossip – circulates the information, so that whatever unit he arrives at, the prisoners there will already be primed to receive him with hostility. One of the most poignant moments I remember was in Healthcare. I spoke to William, who was lying in a half-darkened room with serious injuries to his face and upper torso. He had been convicted of a sex offence but he began to speak to me of his whole life history. He told me that at junior school he had had a really good friend who, as the stronger of the two, had looked out for him. He remembered that as a happy time but, at 11 years old, the two boys were sent to different secondary schools. The lad talking to me said he had then struggled to make friends. As he reached his teens, he longed for a girlfriend, but again found it difficult to form this kind of relationship. By the time he was in his twenties, he found that the only people he could relate to were children, as he identified early childhood as the time when he had been happy. I was blown away by this revelation, as it showed me his reasoning in a completely different way and, even though that he had done something despicable, I felt a little of the compassion of God for him in his loneliness and need. I looked at his injuries and the reason he was lying in a darkened room. He had been very badly scalded on his face and chest, because a fellow prisoner, made aware of his offences, had 'swilled' him – throwing a cup of boiling water, mixed with sugar to make sure it would stick, all over him. William was a red-head and so very fair-skinned. The staff told me that as he was walked over to Healthcare from his unit, his skin was literally peeling off as he walked. He must have been in agony. I had no further conversations with him, but that Christmas received a card from him thanking me for listening to him. I felt very humbled.

If we dwelt on what one person might do to a fellow human being, the darkness might feel too black to fathom. Perhaps in prison we see the depths of depravity; we observe all the darkness that may be present in a person. We see what human nature is really capable of, and have to turn away as we realise that human nature belongs to each one of us. Here we really do come face to face with the true dreadfulness of sin. As we plumb these depths, we have to look at ourselves and appreciate that there is an awful potential in each of us for the same wickedness. Prisoners are very good at putting their fellow inmates into an order of 'worse than me' or 'better than me' but, in God's sight, who is the 'most evil'? Surely the message of the gospel is that none of us can count ourselves righteous before God – we are all in the same place, needing the mercy of God.

I found working in prison a very humbling experience because as I had the privilege to share with these lads – even those who had done such terrible things – I found in my heart an ability to take them as they were, where they were, because of the sense of the love that God still has for them as part of His creation. I do not believe that God in any way condones their wrongdoing, but I also believe that God does not condemn and, in his love for every one of His created children, demands a turning away from wrong – whether a serious crime or just a 'little mistake'. And I have to seek the same in my own life, rather than compare myself to others.

Pause for reflection

In the light of what has been discussed in this chapter, consider the following questions: Do I find myself comparing myself to others and placing people above or below me in an order of merit? Am I prepared to admit that there is darkness in my own life? Could I come to believe that in God's sight we are all undeserving of grace but only receive it through His mercy?

Prayer

Lord, help me as I struggle with this one. Forgive my unwillingness to forgive others who have wronged me or other people. Help me to see others as You see them, and to leave the judgment and reprisals to You. Help me to concentrate on keeping myself in the light and in a place of humility, as I see again that I so often offend against You and others. Lord, in the darkness of those who are paying for their actions in prison, please send Your light of revelation, and Your hope of true reconciliation. Amen.

CHAPTER 9

Regret, Remorse and Repentance

The difference between them
and the consequences

'How long will you refuse to humble yourself before me?'

Exodus 10:3

During the early morning Inductions, I would fairly frequently see men struggling to control their emotions in an attempt to retain their macho image. Possibly, as I am a female, they were more able to let down their guard to me. So often, as I questioned them about their parents or girlfriends, their eyes would begin to fill with tears. Occasionally they would break down completely and we would tactfully remove our 'weeper' to a quiet room to afford them the dignity of privacy. Many of these men were very 'sorry' to be in prison. The word 'sorry' seemed to have a plethora of meanings, and the lads' understanding of their own emotions was probably not the same as mine.

There were always a few prisoners who would loudly declare their innocence or would tell me that they had been 'stitched up'. Of course, there are people who end up in prison having committed no crime, but this is rare. Still, we are faced with the prisoners' perception of what has led to their imprisonment. I remember Andrew who was so mortified at being in prison, accused of raping his girlfriend. Although estranged, she had invited him round and they had slept together in what he had thought was an act of love but, in the morning, she reported him to the police. What tore him to pieces was not being accused of something he had not done, but the fact that he thought they had acted out of love. In court a few months later, he was found 'not guilty' and released. Other men tell me that they take the 'rap' for another member of their family, often a son or girlfriends, and I can believe that in some cases. They tell chaplains these things, but rarely speak of it to others, quietly serving their sentences as unobtrusively as possible. Those who really are innocent and have been wrongly sentenced do not usually make a fuss or declare their innocence; they tend to suffer in silence.

Those who robustly declare their innocence even though proved guilty do run into problems as their sentence progresses. If they are to be released, their sentence planning requires them to attend certain courses – but this presupposes an admission of guilt. If they defend their innocence, they do not wish to attend such courses, as by so doing they are declaring themselves in need of addressing offending behaviour. In these cases, parole will automatically be denied them until they are shown to have addressed their 'offending behaviour'. Occasionally, a prisoner might be acquitted after new evidence comes to light, but this is a rare occurrence.

On a slightly different note, there is also the conundrum of prisoners who were given an Indeterminate Public Protection sentence – a sentence which was introduced several years ago as a measure to ensure that prisoners were not released back into the community if it was felt that they still showed any likelihood of being a danger to the public. Initially, such prisoners were given a minimum tariff of sentence length, which was to be reviewed as their imprisonment progressed. It included conditions such as attending certain courses before parole could be considered. Unfortunately, the number of prisons where such courses were offered were limited and, as these sentences continued to be imposed, so the waiting lists for such establishments became longer. In the last few years I have encountered men who had a tariff of 18 months who were still in prison nine years later. The problem is that the longer they remain in prison, the more difficult it becomes for people to judge just how dangerous they still are and to finally allow them to be released after all this institutionalisation. One of the lads who attended our Living with Loss course had been in prison from his teens and had already been in for over twenty years. Diagnosed with a personality disorder, he had spent time in special units which had not 'counted' towards his tariff, and following this no one seemed to be willing to give him a chance on the outside after so long inside. He was transferred to our prison and I am pleased to say that from us he moved on to a less secure prison. Hopefully, one day, he will be released. His case underlines again the fact that many prisoners are affected with mental health issues and other personality disorders which mean that their coping ability is limited. Left to fend for themselves on the outside, they may well not manage.

Many prisoners are sorry that they have ended up in prison, but are they just sorry they have been caught? Many definitely regret what they have done but, again, is this just because they are now being punished? They speak of their 'moment of madness' or 'the red mist'. I have already mentioned the fact that many of the lads appear to have limited recall of the actual events that led to their imprisonment, as they were under the influence of drink or drugs. Whether or not this is also self-determined as a method of abrogating responsibility for their actions is very difficult to judge. But, just sometimes, the regret and remorse felt by some men is absolute as, in the cold light of day, they realise they must live with what they have done.

Tony was a detoxing alcoholic who was very tearful. He told me he felt bad about hurting the people he loved – his mother and brother. He couldn't remember what he had actually done, as he had been so drunk. He also told me of the many methods he had already employed in an attempt to end his life – taking an overdose, driving into a river (police had rescued him) and then jumping, fully clothed into the river – but he floated. I did point out that perhaps he was meant to be here! Brian had assaulted his girlfriend and he too was feeling really guilty about this and feeling he couldn't live with himself. For men who have committed serious acts of violence, guilt is a sentence in itself to add to the prison sentence. And, unlike many prison sentences, guilt has a habit of carrying on indefinitely. Interestingly, as I have spoken to lads about the potential of receiving God's forgiveness, they can accept this reasonably readily, but they struggle with the ability to forgive themselves. For some, the incarceration is trivial because it can never take away the deep regret that they will have to live forever.

Let me finish Paul's story, the man I mentioned in an early chapter who gave me the poem 'The Cross in my Pocket' because I had treated him 'at face value'.

He had killed his wife, but there were found to be extenuating circumstances – he had been her carer but she had abused him. Unable to cope, he had snapped. He had a comparatively short prison sentence, which reflected the complex nature of the situation. He was a model prisoner and undertook everything required of him. He showed remorse and regret for all he had done. At the halfway point of his sentence, he was released back into the community under licence to complete the sentence. Again, he behaved impeccably and completed all that was required of him. On the day that his licence had been fully served, he left a note and then walked into the river and drowned himself. His note said that he felt that he had repaid his debt to society but that he could no longer live with himself for what he had done. I still treasure the little card he gave me with the poem on it.

I spoke in my introduction of the murderer who was crying, and also the lad in CSU with the picture of the cross. These two, in my opinion, did show genuine remorse and in fact have been greatly assisted by their time in prison to look at their issues. They have used what they learnt to reach out to others, such as the youngster who ran a marathon for victims of road accidents. They cannot undo what they have done nor ease the suffering of the family of the victim, and this is a massive burden of guilt but, in giving to others, they have attempted to try and 'pay back' a little. The whole initiative of 'restorative justice' is based on this premise.

I believe that the biggest turning point comes when the heart is changed, as well as the head. Many prisoners do want to get their lives 'sorted out' and leave prison with very good intentions, which may or may not bear fruit. Often, because they return to their old territory, they are faced with the same domestic uncertainties and the same people who know them as they were and expect them to behave as they did before. Often ex-offenders are fine until something difficult happens. Then they tend to resort to their default response, which may well involve drink or drugs to enable them to cope.

However, from time to time we do see lads whose lives are dramatically changed – and that happens when God intervenes at the deepest level, bringing about a profound inner change. Another lad called Paul came on to our Living with Loss course because he had experienced bereavements in his life. At the end of it, he made the comment that the course had brought him back to his faith. His story was quite amazing. It turned out that he had a grandmother who used to take him to chapel and had prayed for him for years. Paul had been extremely ill and nearly died from a burst oesophagus. As he lay on the sofa in agony, he almost instinctively cried out to God, 'If you show me what is wrong, I will give my life to you.' At that moment, he spurted out a lot of blood and was rushed to hospital where they saved his life. Once he was better he forgot about his promise to God and ended up in prison on quite serious charges. After Living with Loss, he took a Bible back to his cell. One day, he was on the loo, and he had this Bible with him. Often the toilet is the only private place if you share a very small cell. He said he felt a voice telling him to look at a certain page number in the Bible. When he checked it he found the Hebrews 2:3: 'How shall we escape if we ignore so great a salvation?' He immediately felt convicted by this verse as he remembered the promise he had made to God. At that moment he surrendered his life to God again.

The inner transformation in Paul was simply amazing, and it soon became obvious to his fellow prisoners. His past offences were drug-related, and he was an important man in the 'pecking order'. As such, he had always commanded respect from his peers, but now this admiration was obnoxious to him. He told the other lads what had happened to him; that he was no longer the 'boss', but served a higher boss – God. He told me that he couldn't bear to be anywhere near the drugs which were on the unit, as the very smell of them nauseated him. In the past, he would have been using them alongside the others. His behaviour and demeanour so changed that even the prison officers noted it, and also the very calm way he took a transfer to another prison. In the past this might have provoked a violent outburst. God did a very deep work in that young man, and I believe that when he gets out of prison he will be able to live a life away from crime.

A few months after this, another young man, Nick, found a similar sort of faith. I had been to see him when he had been put on an ACCT booklet. He had been angry at having been put on Basic and so had decided to hurt himself by refusing to take his meds. This also meant that he could not eat. In the night when he could not sleep, he had taken out the book *The Monster Within*, by Brian Greenaway, that we gave him on Induction and had read it – and had found God. He said he had so identified with the man who wrote the book and had asked God for His forgiveness. I was somewhat surprised, but talked to him for a while, marvelling that in my capacity as an ACCT Assessor I had been 'sent' to the right person at the right time. He said the last time he had talked like this about faith was to Rev Noel Proctor in Strangeways. I returned with a Bible for Nick, and his quest for more of God was quite amazing. For the next week or so, he kept turning up at the chapel asking for more Christian books. Just like Paul, his face had changed and seemed to be lit up from within. He started to attend Chapel, but it was his change in attitude that was so remarkable. As I spoke to him, he said that one of his fellow prisoners had told him there was a nonce on the unit. Normally this would have produced a very robust negative response, but this time he told the lad that it didn't affect him and he would be speaking to the 'Big Man' about it. He then said to me that he couldn't believe that someone from the Scottie Road in Liverpool could say something like that!

As he carried on reading books, he said he couldn't believe all the similarities he found between those who wrote these things and himself. He likened himself to being like a big snake which had finally shed its skin and begun a new life. He seemed to have an amazing understanding of the Bible although he had never been taught it, and the expressions he used were theological. It was as though God Himself was teaching him, or maybe it was because in times past he had spent time in CSU – with a Bible. All this spilt over into his attitudes about his own personal circumstances. He admitted that he had deliberately put himself back into prison because he could see that he was close to returning to his drug habit. He had expected a short sentence, but got a lot more than he anticipated. Instead of reacting angrily, he saw it in a positive light, and did not react as he would have done in the past. He continued to grow into a new way of regarding those who were sex offenders. As he chatted to them after chapel, he told them that they 'all had the same post code, but just lived in different blocks of houses'.

Nick was a 'likable rogue' and a born raconteur. He turned up one day to ask for a new wooden cross. He said that because he was still on suicide watch, he was being visited by officers on a regular basis. One day he had put a blanket over his head as it was his hour of prayer. In his hand he had the wooden cross I had given him, and he was handling it with his thumbs as he prayed. The officers looked in and mistakenly thought he was texting on a mobile phone and rushed in. Nick put the cross in his pocket so as not to lose it, but they took it from him and, in the process, it got snapped. He showed me the cross, lovingly mended with Elastoplast, which I felt was rather a significant sight. Another time he had been taken to CSU for an adjudication for an offence he had supposedly committed. He told the officers he was a 'lost case like Jesus Christ, because they chose to believe Barabbas'. He got let off! He was later transferred to another prison to complete his sentence and I pray that he will continue to grow in grace because God has clearly started a deep work within him.

Because of the transitory nature of our prison population, it is often hard to see the results of our sharing the word of God with these men. So much of what we do is the casual conversation as we pass by, and we may never see that particular person again. We have to believe that the seeds we plant may eventually come to fruition – our task is to be faithful in the sowing. The men face many difficulties in being ready to repent and in changing heart as well as mind. We believe that it is by the grace and strength of God alone that true rehabilitation takes place.

Those men that do get out of prison and do not re-offend show enormous amounts of perseverance and self-motivation. With some it comes as a conse-quence of their maturity; they say things like, 'I'm getting too old for this now, Miss. I've been coming to prison since I was a teenager.' Some have to break away from their previous environment and branch out in a new place with new acquain-tances and circumstances. When one stops to consider the damage that has so often been done to these men before they come to prison – their dysfunctional parenting, their violent backgrounds and their own poor life choices – one has to admit that it would be an uphill struggle for even the most capable person. That is why I believe that when a man opens himself to the enabling power of God to transform him from within, he begins to have the inner strength and wisdom that can begin to guide him in the right direction for the rest of his life.

Pause for reflection

Do we regret what we have done in the past?

Do we feel remorse for wrong actions or are we able to find justification for them?

Are there times when, although we have felt sorry for what we have done, we have not felt ready to turn away from it and move in a different direction?

Prayer

Father, we are sorry for the things we have done that have hurt You and others. We know how easy it is to justify what we have done. Teach us to look at Your cross often, and see what you have forgiven us and so change the way we live. Amen.

CHAPTER 10

The Revolving Door

The problems of resettlement
and real rehabilitation

'I have come that they may have life, and have it to the full.'

John 10:10

In the first few years of my work in Chaplaincy, we kept a fairly simple index card system detailing a few personal notes about each prisoner as we spoke to them on Induction, and then adding to it if they came to see us again, for example at a times of bereavement. Every time a man returned to us we would get out his 'old card' and add to it, or we would start a new card and clip the entries together. In this way, we quickly became aware of the number of men who do return to prison – time and time again. I used to joke with one man that I had so many cards about him that I could soon be playing a game of patience with a full pack! He was someone who would be out for a few months but then, having failed to find a permanent address, would usually end up on the streets again. Homelessness might result in him committing a crime. Always cheerful and resigned to his way of life, Derek accepted prison as a way of life between places of residence.

Some men came in and out of prison for years. Most had no family or other support. They usually lived alone and resorted to alcohol as a way of keeping warm and reasonably happy. Causing upset as a result of drink, they would pick up ASBOs as a consequence. In the old days, they would have been termed 'gentlemen of the road'. When I first came to prison, I remember a man being brought in because he had been found with less than £1 in his pocket which constituted the offence of 'vagrancy' – a law that is still in force today, though due to be repealed.

Jimmy was an amazing example of such a man. He came to us quite regularly and was so interesting. He was also quite a skilled artist and, once settled back into prison, was often seen at a table with pencil and paper. Over the years, he told me bits about himself. He was very much at home in the outdoors, and had a tent, although it sometimes got stolen. At one time, he told me he had hidden the tent in a hollow tree trunk in the middle of a wood, so as to keep it safe. He appeared to be well-known to his local community and, one Christmas when he returned to us, he told me he had been offered several Christmas dinners by his neighbours. I could understand this, as on a good day he was very pleasant and sociable. In fact, he told me of an amazing encounter he had had with someone who also appeared to appreciate him. Jimmy had been walking along the road when a very posh car drew up alongside him, and a famous footballer who lived locally got out to speak to him. He asked Jimmy if he knew him, and Jimmy replied that he did. The footballer told him he knew who Jimmy was and had seen him from time to time. He wanted to help Jimmy because Jimmy was not drunk that day. The footballer gave him a signed photograph of himself and told Jimmy to put it on eBay and use the money that he would get from it. When Jimmy recounted this to me, I was secretly amused at the thought that Jimmy would have a computer and internet connection in a tent in the middle of a wood! But Jimmy was a very enterprising individual, and what he did completely surprised me. He took the signed photograph to the local newspaper, asked them to put it on eBay – and give the money received to the NSPCC! This story is not the sort of thing that would normally get into the press, because it puts prisoners in a favourable light but, as we will see later, the ethical world of a prisoner is a complex affair.

Ethan was also a 'frequent flier', and for years lived almost permanently with us. As soon as he was released he would be back again. He had all sorts of health issues, as he was not young. He had a hernia on his stomach which he liked to show to people. After a while, I used to forestall him as I saw him going to lift up his T-shirt to show it to me! Because he had become so institutionalised it was very difficult to find a place for him on the outside. He was notorious in his locality and there were not many places willing to take him. Finally, he was placed in a hostel and he continued to write to us for a while, telling us of his daily routine. After a few months this ceased, and what became of him we will never know.

One of the hardest things about prison is the yawning gap between the inside and outside of the institution. Staff in prison seek to help every single prisoner who comes through the doors but, with their diversity of needs, this is a herculean task. Because so many prisoners are in prison for such a short period of time, and the programmes run are designed for the 'average' prisoner, there are clearly many people whose needs are not met. Youngsters who have evaded most of their mainstream schooling are often still not motivated to study, even if forced to do so, and the older men often resent having to return to 'school' when in their own lives, they have 'grafted with their hands' and got by on their own wit. Many of them have taught themselves to read and write what they require. So although we may ensure that prisoners are educated in some way whilst in prison, this does not in any way guarantee them a successful job when they leave, especially after only a few weeks inside. They then return to their communities and their old patterns of life, and often quickly reoffend. One of the only advantages of giving such men constant short periods of internment is that for the sake of their neighbourhoods – for a few short weeks they are removed from the society where they have caused distress.

One of the main reasons why people come back to prison is that they have never really conquered the addictions that have ruled their lives, often for many years. In prison, every prisoner has the chance to engage with a detox programme, but not all choose to do so. When I started in prison, there was no methadone programme, and so prisoners had to come off drugs straightaway, whether or not they wished to do so, but we now have a well-organised methadone programme so that prisoners may still detox completely if they wish, or may stabilise so that they are still on a dose of methadone when they leave prison. Some prisoners who are really motivated take every opportunity afforded to them in prison to make the break away from their environment to reorientate their lives, and some of them do achieve this. Those who are in for the first time are fast-tracked as soon as possible to get them suitable support and onto programmes, because the chance of then not reoffending is much greater. We have regular AA and NA meetings in prison so that these men can start to belong to a group that they can continue to attend on the outside.

Increasingly we are seeing the need for other support groups, as illustrated by Charlie, who stayed behind to talk to me after Induction. As I talked to him about his background, which was more normal than most, and the fact that he was educated and had had a good job, I began to wonder just how he had landed up in jail. An inner voice prompted me to ask him, 'Do you have a problem with gambling?' At this point, his face changed completely and he told me that during of the course of one weekend he had lost over £100,000 gambling on the internet. His subsequent crime was committed in an effort to recoup this horrendous loss. He later said that until that point he had never admitted to anyone, including himself, that he had a problem with gambling. He was one of the first men who attended our newly formed GA (Gamblers Anonymous) group. With gambling opportunities now being so readily available, on the street and increasingly the internet, more and more people are being drawn into this habit, which can rapidly take hold.

I wonder, too, if society also needs to consider the issue of sexual addictions, which may well be linked to the rise of porn being so readily available in people's homes. In every case an addiction starts when people do something habitually and think they are in charge of it, but after a while the addiction takes hold of them and they are unable to let go of it. One lad said to me, 'My head wants to give up the heroin, but my body won't let me.' To overcome addiction and find true freedom is a very long uphill struggle from a human point of view. Again, if these lads do find faith, I believe they then have the power of God at their disposal. The battle may still wage, but they have His inner strength.

Whilst we try to address the offending behaviour whilst prisoners are on the inside and prepare them to return to the outside, the reality is that the whole system is totally overwhelmed. In my opinion, it would seem more efficient to give offenders a longer minimum sentence of at least a year to serve in jail, so that we would have sufficient time to look at their individual needs and give them the help they need to really make their future lives different. We also need to see some more forms of 'halfway houses' for longer-term offenders as they leave prison, so that for a few months they could live in community with additional support, away from their unhelpful associates, and be encouraged back by degrees into a job and their own accommodation. At the moment, their first stop is at a hostel, which does work for some but, more often is the place where they can obtain drugs and set off again on the path of reoffending. If we were able to set up more independent community type initiatives, with prisoners being able to work together on projects such as recycling/upcycling to sustain their community, there might be more likelihood of a sea change. Clearly the cost implications are enormous, but weighed against the cost of readmitting men to prison on multiple occasions, it could well prove its worth in the long run.

There have been various schemes across the country of Community Chaplaincy, which runs in parallel with the Chaplaincy in prison. The idea is that people from the community – mainly from church backgrounds – come into the prison's visiting area to meet prisoners before they are released. After release, the Community Chaplains arrange to meet the men in a neutral place, such as a coffee shop, on a regular basis so they can keep an eye on them and make sure they get to appointments etc. The idea is that they offer support in much the same way as we do as Chaplains in prison – with no strings attached, as to church attendance or belief. This is a wonderful idea, but it is fraught with difficulties, notwithstanding being very labour intensive. With increasing understanding of public protection issues, there needs to be a robust safety net for those volunteering, as ex-offenders take time to reacclimatise to the 'norms' of the outside and often come with a great deal of baggage from the past, which affects their attitudes and actions. With the numbers of prisoners going in and out of jail, the logistics of 'support tracking' everyone who leaves prison would be very difficult. As with the idea of halfway houses, the cost of setting up such systems is enormous but, in light of our ever-increasing prison population, it is something that needs to be considered.

The role of the local church in such initiatives is also a difficult issue. If we believe that God can truly forgive even the worst offenders and offer them a new life of grace, then how can we not welcome them into our churches? However, we have to consider the safety of others in the church, especially vulnerable people. The idea of welcoming past sex offenders into a worshipping community has obvious risks. Many churches have adopted structures to allow them to welcome such people, with a monitored system. There may be problems with welcoming other ex-offenders – for example, burglars. Would we be happy for them to take responsibility in the church? This whole topic constitutes a very difficult conundrum – how can we, on the one hand, offer loving care and acceptance to all in the name of Christ but, on the other hand, be realistic about the possible pitfalls?

In my work as a Chaplain, I was very aware that as we walk among all sorts of people, most of whom have never had any kind of contact with the Church, that we take the presence of Christ with us. We do indeed walk among the mad, the bad and the sad – just as Jesus did, as he spoke to marginalised people on the roadside. When I look at the Gospels, I see that so much of Jesus' teaching wasn't just in the synagogue, but in the fields. I often used to say to the prisoners, 'Whom did Jesus condemn?' We would examine the Word and see that it was usually only those who thought they had got it all right, such as the Pharisees and Sadducees. Jesus spent so much 'quality' time with people who had got it horribly wrong in the world's eyes – the leprous, the maimed, the woman caught in adultery and, at the very end, the thief on the cross. This made me humbly aware that I could see people in the way Jesus saw them – as they are, warts and all! When I met people individually and listened to their stories, I often felt such a deep compassion for them that I felt had to be God-given. I do believe that just as with the woman caught in adultery, Jesus does not condemn people, but he also does not condone the wrong that they do. He told the woman to 'go and sin no more'. And that was why I constantly challenged those with whom I spoke, about changing their lives and attitudes, so that they could find a life really worth living.

But marrying the quiet talks in the chapel in prison with the context of a local church is hard. Men who do find some meaning to faith in prison may not yet be ready for the arrangements in a local church, or sure enough of what they believe to engage in groups.

Men tell me that on the outside they have sometimes tried to go to a local church as they have been passing, but it has often been locked. It is often hard for any newcomer to brave church, but when one has just been 'inside' it is perhaps much more difficult. A few churches have managed to set up groups just for ex-offenders, so that they can gradually be integrated into church life, but these seem fairly thin on the ground. In the midst of all the other things that happen in a church, these groups may not be given a high priority because of limited resources.

A final story to illustrate my point is perhaps the most difficult of all to write about. Bernard was a priest in the Church of England, who had committed a downloading offence. We talked honestly about his crime and he told me that he had been relieved to be caught, and actually asked to go to prison so that he could break away from his wrongdoing. His sentence was short, but he was visited by a senior churchman during his incarceration. At the end of his sentence the priest was put on a sex offenders' register for five years. He then received a letter from the Church saying that his case would be reviewed in 20 years' time. He was absolutely devastated by this. He left prison to a very uncertain future, having lost not only his vocation, but also his job and his home. When I asked what support network there was for those in his position, he knew of none. I struggled with this one – weighing up, as one should, the safety of others and the responsibility of being a clergyperson, with the man's own need as a human being for forgiveness and restoration through the infinite grace of God.

Reoffending and rehabilitation are massive issues and not ones that are easily managed. We do live in a fractured society, where moral and ethical values have fragmented over the years. The family, as an integrated unit, has gradually been eroded, and we are faced with the consequences of this, as we witness more and more broken lives and dysfunctional relationships. Our present society has become very materialistic and hedonistic, and the individual's need for God appears to be much less relevant in their eyes. I found it interesting that when I started in prison 14 years ago, about a third of the prison registered as Church of England, a third were Roman Catholic and a third were Nil (with just a sprinkling of other faiths). By the time I left, Church of England and the Roman Catholics were down to less than a fifth each, and about 60 percent of prisoners were registering as Nil religion. We also noted that most of the men under the age of 30 were in this latter category, apart from a few retaining their Roman Catholic allegiance. For the young lads, religion was just not relevant to their everyday lives. And yet even these, given a bereavement, would nearly all opt to come to the chapel if they were not allowed to attend a funeral – because it was 'there' and open to them. Most of them welcomed prayer when offered, and nearly all of them lit a candle. The Church did have something to offer them which no one else could at this most vulnerable time.

In the outside world, in our churches, we also see the challenges of maintaining and sustaining our current, often aging congregations and being relevant and accessible to the 'unchurched' younger generation, which has been raised in a completely different way. Trying to get these worlds to meet is difficult. So much more so to meet the needs of the very marginalised in our society, not only ex-offenders but also those with chronic mental health issues and addictions that live in our parishes. There is no easy solution. The subject requires much prayer and wisdom as we continue to try and live differently in a secular world that presses around us.

Pause for reflection

Do we persistently bring our broken and dysfunctional society to God, and pray for a true breaking through with the relevance of the gospel to 'modern man'?
How can we reach out to marginalised people in our vicinity – meet them where they are and be with them when they need us?
How do we respond to those who have done terrible things but now want to live in a different way alongside us?

Prayer

Father, we pray for those who are caught in the loop of reoffending because they find it so hard to establish themselves and find stability and support in their lives. Forgive us that we find it so easy to criticise those who have offended. Help us to have Your heart of love and hope for them, that You do promise new life to all who put their trust in You. Amen.

PART THREE
Moving On

CHAPTER 11

Living with Loss

Dealing with bereavement in all its forms and learning to move on

He heals the brokenhearted and binds up their wounds.

Psalm 147:3

When I first started to work as a chaplain, I met many prisoners who were detoxing from drugs or alcohol. Years ago, we offered no substitute treatment, so the prisoners really had to go 'cold turkey' and come off substances completely. Whilst I expected to hear screams of anguish on the Detox Unit, most of the inmates seemed to suffer in silence – taking to their beds for a few days until the worst of the effects had taken place. A few weeks on, as I chatted to them, I was amazed at how pleasant and normal they were when in their 'right minds'. They not only responded better verbally, but they looked about ten years younger than when they had first arrived in prison (they liked it when I told them that!). I began to ask them why they had started on the destructive downward spiral of drink and drugs in the first place, and I fully expected them to tell me that they had succumbed to peer pressure. To my amazement – and dare I say shame – most of the replies were not about 'mates' but about bereavement. 'I started to take drugs when my nan died… when my best mate took an overdose… when my mum committed suicide and I found her… when my baby died…'

It slowly occurred to me that death is not something that many of us speak about – it is something that we are expected to cope with and 'move on' from.

Every one of us has to suffer bereavement at some point; it is part of life. With family and friends around us, many of us do come through it. But if your support network is unstable and dysfunctional and not coping at all well with 'normal' life themselves, how much less are they able to help someone who is bereaved? And the reality is that if there is no support, one of the easiest ways to cope is to attempt to obliterate the pain with drugs or drink. They become an anaesthetic which eases the pain for a little because it numbs all senses.

Many of the men I met had experienced loss on a grand scale. I was told horrendous stories of the loss of family members who had been in fires, road accidents, a child who was burned on a cooker, a nephew who had been electrocuted. Nick told me that his baby had died from lupus, yet he and his partner had been accused of not feeding the child properly. And then there were the suicides, which tended to run in families. One prisoner would be told one week that his brother had taken his own life in another jail and, three weeks later, another brother did the same on the outside of prison. Dominic and his girlfriend had lost a baby and then the girlfriend committed suicide. Ben's mum had died from an overdose of heroin and then his sister was in hospital on the brink of death for the same reason. For some men, the list seemed extreme: Nick had lost his baby, his father and a mate, and wanted to know, 'Why does God allow it?' On the other hand, Rob had lost a mate who fought alongside him in Afghanistan, and said he had never thought of God before but was willing to pray. Vernon, who attended our Living with Loss course, said that he had had 18 bereavements in two years, and would no longer pick up the phone at home for fear it might be someone giving him bad news.

Two particularly sad stories have remained with me over the years, and both concerned young daughters. I received a phone call from Mark's father, who wanted to tell him that his daughter, Bethany, aged three, had just been diagnosed with cancer. She had had a childhood illness which had not cleared up and, after a scan in hospital, a tumour had been discovered. We took Mark into a manager's office so he could speak to his father. When he had received the news, his mother asked to speak to me. I will never forget her words: 'Will you please look after Mark; he has already lost two children.' It transpired that Mark had had twin baby boys, both of whom died – one at birth and one shortly after. He was only 22 years old. We supported Mark as he waited on news of the outcome of an operation on Bethany. She came through the operation successfully, and I was able to give him that news. But, the next day, I received another stricken telephone call from Mark's father – Bethany had died. I shall never forget the walk I took to Mark's unit. My heart was so heavy, and I felt so reluctant to have to be the bearer of such terrible news. What was worse, was that he was already at the door to his unit, anxious for an update. I shall never forget how his face fell when I said he needed to come upstairs to speak to his dad on the phone, who told him the worst. My heart was so full of compassion as Mark listened on the phone. I prayed that God would somehow give him strength and comfort beyond what human sympathy we could offer. When Mark finally spoke, he said to me, 'Katy, I'm glad she died whilst I was in prison. When the twins died, I just hit the bottle.' He was due out of prison very shortly after that, and the hospital where Bethany had died arranged to keep her body so that upon release he could say his final goodbye.

Stuart had never been in prison before and came to us just after one Christmas. He had two children – a little girl aged three and a lad aged six years. He was separated from their mum and the children lived with her. One morning, the children were up and playing downstairs before the mum got up. The little girl got hold of a bottle of perfume and poured it all over herself. Somehow, a match was lit, and she literally went up in flames. She spent the next three months in a children's hospital having multiple skin grafts. Stuart said she looked like a mummy as he sat with her at her bedside through that time. But, in spite of her treatment, she died, and Stuart was devastated. He was offered counselling, but there was a waiting list and so he just went out and drank. The reason for him being in prison that he had gone to a pub just before Christmas and police were checking the alcohol levels of people returning to their cars. In his inebriated state, Stuart hit one of the police officers. Whilst never condoning violence in any shape or form, it is hard not to feel compassion for a person in such a terrible position, and to ask questions about the lack of support offered to him.

It was Michael who finally challenged me into action, to care for those who have suffered such unbearable losses. He told me that he had lost his mother to cancer and his wife in a road traffic accident in the space of two months. He had also lost several other family members that year. He felt low and took himself to his local GP who told him he was 'the saddest man he had ever met'. He was referred for counselling but then told he was 'too depressed' to engage with it. He found his solace in drink, which was what led to him ending up in prison. It was stories such as these that inspired me to set up the bereavement course Living with Loss, which we ran three times a year over a fairly long period of time. I felt that if people did not deal with the underlying problems which led them to drink, it would be extremely difficult to break free from the addiction.

The course material originated in a prison in the South of England. I took their outline and adapted it. Over time, my Roman Catholic colleague and I, who jointly ran the course, said that no two courses were ever the same – the format varied according to the needs and abilities of the group. We tried to keep any requirement for the prisoners to read or write to a minimum, so that no one would be deterred from attending. Interestingly, we found that in some groups word searches were a useful tool in promoting discussion, as they gave us key words that we could explore with the men. If you ask a group of people how they feel about loss, it requires a certain level of vocabulary and articulation to explore the subject, but word searches offered a way into discussion.

Every week on the course we would show a TV or film clip, and this was also useful in promoting discussion. The course was not overtly Christian, and the clips came from sitcoms such as *One Foot in the Grave* and *Steptoe and Son*. They helped us to look at others' attitudes to death and dying.

As the weeks went by on each course, the men would get to know each other and begin to share not only their life histories and losses, but also their emotions. For many men, it does not come naturally to confess to feelings of anger, guilt, regret or confusion. It requires a degree of courage and a sense of safety and confidentiality. Whilst my colleague and I did give some input and steered the conversations, I felt that the most valuable part of the course was the support and mutual understanding that developed between the men as they began to trust each other. It is a tribute to the structure of the course that, on several occasions at the end of it, the men wished to continue meeting with each other!

We deliberately described the course as not just a bereavement course. The title Living with Loss reminded the men that loss can come in many forms. Those in prison have often lost a great deal, particularly in terms of relationships. We have spoken already of dysfunctional families and the pain of losing a child to fostering or adoption. I will never forget the time I spent with Adrian in the chapel. He was one of the most miserable prisoners I have ever met, and with reason. He had already had one of his children taken into care, and then faced the threat of losing another. He was absolutely distraught and would not stop crying. I was at my wits' end as to what to say to him. I went out of the chapel to make him a cup of coffee, in an attempt to take his mind, at least temporarily, somewhere else. When I returned to the chapel, he was nowhere to be seen and, for one awful moment, I thought he might have hidden himself somewhere and 'strung himself up'. I finally located him on the floor under the radiator, in the foetal position, just howling. I don't remember how I finally got him through this agony, but the picture of such distress will remain imprinted on my mind for ever.

Losses which drive men to seek comfort in drink and drugs are added to as their lives start to disintegrate. Many become homeless and jobless, have no money and lose all their friends. Others are damaged through accidents and other mishaps. Barry spoke of his feelings about being adopted and also losing the sight in one eye due to an unfortunate self-inflicted injury. Frank, who had been serving in the army, had suffered a horrific accident with a tank which had left him with a facial disfigurement and loss of part of his tongue. Paul had lived in 28 hostels and William had had to have both his legs amputated due to emphysema. Whilst not bereavements, the emotions surrounding these losses were similar to those experienced when a loved one dies. The breakdown of relationships, especially when the girlfriend or partner had rejected them, often felt like a 'living' bereavement, and was even more painful when the partner became involved with another.

Over the weeks, we would first look at emotions in general, then go on to the two difficult topics of anger and guilt. Anger is never far from the surface in many of the lads that I have met, and I believe that in many cases, the spring of that anger is buried deep in hurts, usually from way back in childhood. If a child is hurt physically, mentally or emotionally when they are young, they cannot fight back on an equal level – they are too small and weak. It seems to me that this hurt then gets packed away, but not dissipated, and as the child grows up the hurt is like an unerupted volcano within them. Given the right set of stimuli, one day the volcano explodes and, if fuelled by alcohol or drugs, can have catastrophic results. When the men have calmed down and think, they realise that this is what happens, but often the response is so ingrained within them, that it is very hard for them to change. This is particularly true when they have been reared in a violent environment and witnessed all types of anger from a very early age. When someone they love dies, it is as though that deep well of hurt is touched yet again; they are rejected again because of the death of that person who has 'left them'. As Chaplains, whenever we have to relay the news of a death or serious illness to a prisoner, we always take them into the privacy of a manager's office, so that if they do react with anger, they can do so without having an audience to add to their misery. I have had lads storm out of the room when I have given them bad news, and one of my colleagues had a man try to throw things around the room. I must admit that more often than not the men will break down and cry, possibly because they feel they can do so in the presence of a woman, but I am always relieved to see that outward expression of grief, rather than a stony and apparently disinterested silence that sometimes may occur.

Frank, who came to one of our courses, described himself as 'a rusty nail, with all the bitterness of years'. As we discuss anger and all its associated emotions and behaviours, we look at how we may try to diffuse these very strong feelings. The concept of 'anger dumping' is explored – those times when pent-up feelings get unleashed on someone else. Often the recipients of this violence are those nearest and dearest to us. This resonates with many prisoners, and I remember Vernon, who had had so many bereavements, suddenly grasping this as a 'light bulb' moment. He never returned to prison again, although he had been a persistent offender for years. The prisoners collectively put forward ideas to diffuse their anger in a constructive way – through sport and gym and through creativity in all its forms.

Another strong emotion which many prisoners experience is that of guilt. They will admit that they still feel guilty many years after an event. As they share in this environment, the others can really help and affirm them. Nick had a baby who had severe problems at birth and was put on a life-support machine. He and his girlfriend sat for days with their child. In the end, Nick was called into a room without his girlfriend and told that he had to persuade his girlfriend to allow the machine to be turned off, as the baby would not survive. Nick did as he was told and had never forgiven himself for allowing this to happen. He was just 16 years old at the time. As he told his story, the others in the group gathered around him and told him that he had had no choice - he had done the only thing possible and it was not his fault. He still struggled, but one sensed that he had received a bit of release from a terrible burden. Another lad called Graham had had to turn off his mother's life-support machine when he was only 19 years old. He was left with the responsibility of providing for several younger brothers and sisters. He slipped into crime as a way of providing for his siblings' basic needs of food and water. He felt he had let his mother down and was haunted by the thought that if her life-support machine had not been turned off, she might have lived. I also heard stories of 'survivor's guilt'. Pete had run away from an abusive home situation and his brothers rode to find him. On his journey home with them, they had an accident and Pete's two brothers were killed, but he came out alive. He felt guilty because he had encouraged his brother to get the motorbike on which they had had the fatal accident.

Perhaps most poignant of all, men may be in prison because they have taken the life of another, even if unintentionally. Brian was a diabetic man who had failed to take his insulin the day he took his mother in his car. He suffered a hyperglycaemic attack and crashed the car, which killed his mother. Robert had his young and only son in his car as he travelled home from a birthday party. He overtook a vehicle on a country road and crashed into another car. He survived with only minor injuries, but his son was killed. As a consequence of this accident, Robert had a recurring shoulder problem which the doctors could have treated but he wished to endure as it reminded him daily of his son. He found it really difficult to contemplate letting go of this pain to release himself. In another way, William struggled following his time as a soldier. He felt acutely guilty about the people he had killed and also that he had lost mates in the conflict. As a consequence, he had tried to take his own life. As we talked he said he had realised that he needed God's forgiveness and that giving his life for others was better than throwing it away.

The final week of the course is one which draws together all we have learnt and brings us to a point where the lads can collectively and publicly make a decision to let go of the past and look towards the future. Up to this point, the course has not been overtly Christian, but this last part brings in our hope of redemption and forgiveness through Christ. We start with a simple act of remembrance, when we invite the participants to share their memories of those they have lost in whatever way feels appropriate. We have had poems, songs, tributes, letters and simply a name as we light candles for each of those special people. This is an amazingly poignant moment, and one senses the presence of God in a very real way as the prisoners respond to each other's contributions. I will never forget the moment when Jack, who had been in prison for 30 years (on an original three-year tariff), read out a poem about his mum, who had died whilst he had been in prison. On the other side of the room was Simon, who had been in and out of prison for years and had also lost his mother. Simon started to shake with sobs, and Jack, normally a man of few words, got up and went over and laid his hand on Simon's shoulder and said, 'It's all right; I know how you feel.' It was a truly awesome moment and one felt that healing was present. Other moving contributions from lads were addressed to someone they had lost – often asking them for forgiveness and expressing feelings of guilt and shame. Candles were lit and we committed those who had died to God.

What followed this was every bit as powerful. We talked to them about the difficulty not only of being and feeling forgiven by others, but also of allowing themselves to be forgiven or forgiving themselves. In previous weeks, we had watched excerpts from the film *The Mission*, and looked at how the 'bad lad' took a penance of carrying a heavy burden which he refused to let go of – until he was finally released from it. We then told them the story of the Prodigal Son and the father's love in spite of everything the son had done. We talked about Jesus' death not only dealing with sin but also disease (Isaiah 53:4). We invited them to write down on paper those things they would like to get rid of in their lives and then we put the pieces in a thurible and burnt them with incense as an act of surrender. Nobody knew what anyone else wrote, but this seemed to be very meaningful for them. We had told them the week before that we would be doing this, and Simon came well prepared. He told us he had written his life story and he wanted to burn it all (five pages of file paper!) because he felt that he wanted to 'start again'. Our first thought was that we might set off all the fire alarms in the chapel! However, we agreed to burn it, but in the sink in the kitchen! The next day I met with Simon and he said of the experience, 'It blew me away'. Another lad told me the next day that he felt he had 'been reborn'. I found that an amazing turn of phrase.

On the outside, we encounter the death of others but then are expected to 'get on with life'. All of us experience bereavement at some time or other and may need support and comfort. For those who are in the midst of chaos, dysfunction and violence, such commodities may be in short supply. There are few places readily available to such people that offer personal support or counselling. Kirk came on our Living with Loss course and was really helped by it. He had lost his teenage daughter to a bad dose of heroin. He was inconsolable and turned to drink, which became a real problem and he ended up in prison. Whilst inside he also received some bereavement counselling. When he was released, it was arranged for this to continue whilst he was still in a hostel. All went well to begin with, but then the counsellor went away. Kirk was desperate, as he realised that he could easily lapse back into alcoholism again. He sought help at the only place he knew well – the police station. He asked there for a bereavement counsellor. Perplexed, they said that they couldn't help so, in real distress, Kirk asked if he could go back to prison as he knew he would get a counsellor in there. The police said that he couldn't go back to prison unless he had committed a crime. Kirk went back to the hostel and threw a brick through a window. He was duly arrested and sent back to jail. He succeeded in getting the help he needed, but hardly in the most constructive or rehabilitative way.

If prison numbers are to be decreased, this is another avenue that may be worth pursuing. Can we provide more aftercare for those who have lost loves ones, especially in difficult and tragic circumstances, or must they sink into despair and dependence on substances before their real needs are met?

Pause for reflection

Bereavement is a part of life. What strategies have we developed to cope with loss? Do we deal with all feelings or do we hide some away?

How can we reach out to those who are struggling with loss in a way that is 'user-friendly' and available to those who do not necessarily engage with faith?

Prayer

Father, we thank You that as we look at Jesus we see a knowledge and understanding of suffering in all its forms. Thank You that You can be with us in the darkest places of despair and pain, and You can also take from us the heavy burdens that we often continue to carry. As we experience life-giving hope, may we be aware of all those around us who are suffering and crying out for help, and reach out with Your love and tenderness. Amen.

CHAPTER 12

'Rosemarys' and Footprints
Folk religion in prison and its significance

'And I, when I am lifted up from the earth, will draw all people to myself.'

John 12:32

One of the most frequent request we get on Induction is, 'Miss, can I have one of them rosemarys?' For those who do not work in prison, this may need to be translated. Over the years, prisoners nearly always call a rosary, a rosemary. This may be something to do with the latter part of the word reminding them of the Virgin Mary. For many, it is part of prison life that you possess a set of such beads. Many do have Roman Catholic roots, but for others it is just a 'possession' that they are allowed. Over the years, we have become a little more discriminatory as to our distribution of rosaries, so that they retain some of their spiritual value. We will give them to lads who attend Mass, but otherwise they can purchase them from the 'canteen' list, at a fairly small cost. Their subsequent use varies. For the genuine man, they are worn under his shirt and possibly used appropriately in prayer, but for others they are displayed as a piece of jewellery round their necks, and may be worn in multiples. A few years ago, we were instructed to only supply black or white beads as, in some establishments, prisoners were buying different colours as a sign of specific gang membership. Walking into cells we also often find them draped over photographs or arranged symmetrically over the mirror. If a prisoner has had a bereavement whilst in jail and has received cards or has a funeral service, the beads may well be incorporated into that. Sometimes they are even sent out to family members, especially children.

Attitudes towards religion in prison is interesting and continues to evolve. Increasingly, the vast majority of prisoners have apparently little interest in the spiritual, coming as they do from an increasing materialistic and hedonistic society, and for many of them faith is completely irrelevant. Yet in prison there remains a sort of a residual 'folklore' of faith, and established practices such as the wearing of rosary beads somehow typifies this. Early on I recognised that the possession of something tangible such as rosary beads is helpful to many, and so I found a place that produced small, very cheap holding crosses made of balsa wood. We gave these to many at times of loss (and also put them on the canteen list so they could buy them themselves!). Whatever a man's faith or lack of it, these crosses seemed to be very much appreciated and valued as a symbol. In cells, they were nearly always displayed and often embellished using very ingenious means. Some got stained (probably with coffee) and others were inscribed using pen with names and messages.

Part of the fabric of prison life is the custom that when a prisoner loses someone close to them, they are invited to go to the chapel and light a candle. When we break bad news to a lad, we always mention this opportunity in our conversation, and an amazing number of lads respond and come over to the chapel to 'show their respect'. I am not sure that many of them would so seek a church on the outside at a time like this. The other time that many will come over to chapel is when they are not allowed to go to a funeral. Prison Order rules dictate that, as a normal matter of course, the only funerals that prisoners are permitted to attend are those of close blood relatives. Therefore, this precludes funerals of their mates, whose loss is often felt far more than the loss of an immediate relative. Perhaps even more poignantly, it precludes their grandparents. Time after time we had distraught prisoners in the chapel on such occasions. Raging at the system that had prevented them being with their families at this worst possible time, but often, deep down, consumed by guilt and regret that they have landed themselves in a place where they will yet again be letting down their nearest and dearest. We seek to sit with them and allow them to express their grief. I tried to give them all the time they needed, both to speak and also to have their own time of silence if they wished. Sometimes they really did not want to do anything except light a candle; that was 'it' and they had done what they felt they should do, and they then just wanted to 'escape'. Everyone is different, but on many of these occasions I found that lads would be very open, at this raw time, to look again at themselves and where they were going in life. I used to challenge, especially the youngsters, with the question, 'What do you think your nan/granddad would have said to you if she/he was still here?' And the response was nearly always the same: 'She'd have told me to get off my backside and to sort out my life.' We would then take time to look at some of the practicalities involved in doing just that. At the end of our time, I would always ask if they would like me to pray, and they nearly always responded positively. I suspect that many of them had never been prayed for personally, and they often used to say things like, 'That was lovely, Miss.' As they went I always tried to give them something so that they had a tangible reminder of their time spent in chapel. Apart from the wooden cross, I often gave them a copy of 'Footprints' - that amazing piece that speaks deeply to so many people, about God being there at the difficult times and carrying us. Time and time again, the lads would tell me that they had heard that piece at a funeral, or that Nan had it on her wall at home. I also gave out copies of 'The Serenity Prayer', although I did have to check that they knew what 'serenity' actually meant, as most of them had not heard the word. They understood when I explained it to them.

A scripture I frequently gave to them was from Isaiah 43, reminding them that God does not promise us trouble-free lives, but that every point of suffering is a place where He is always with us. After this, many of them would ask for Bibles and Christian books. Over the years, we have given out so many 'free' books, which have been so kindly donated to us. I have already spoken of the deep effect they can have on some prisoners. Over the years, we received multiple copies of testimonies from various ex-offenders such as *One Step Beyond* by Gram Seed, *To catch a Thief*, by Richard Taylor, and *Once an Addict*, by Barry Woodward. We regularly hosted meetings by the men from 'Tough Talk', who would also leave their books for us. In later years, we received over 3,000 copies of *The Monster Within* from CWR, and so could freely distribute these. This also becomes part of prison life; as lads come through Induction, they receive a Christian book if they wish; brand-new and just for them as individuals. And many of them do read it at some point in their prison life.

We also have an almost endless supply of calendars and diaries given to us. Diaries in particular have become synonymous with chaplaincy and, as the supply gradually runs out just before Christmas, we are constantly badgered by lads on the units for new ones, which we do not distribute until after Christmas to ensure that our annual supply is efficiently shared by all. These diaries have a daily scripture reading but are used by most prisoners as a way of keeping telephone numbers in a handy place and, as such, are highly valued! Whilst maybe not actively leading prisoners into faith, this is another way by which the chaplaincy is known and respected. For many, a time of bereavement was their one and only visit to the chapel, but some did come back again and a few of them came onto the Living with Loss course. Many prisoners also came over on anniversary days, even years down the line. I sat with lads who had lost relatives 30 years before, but always marked the day 'with respect'.

I was also very aware of the burden of guilt many of them carried when they were not allowed to attend funerals and, over the years, have encouraged lads to write something about their loved one which we then send out so that it can be included in the funeral service. Whilst initially most prisoners warm to this idea, I soon realised that may were reluctant to do it because their writing skills were limited. I devised a gentle way of overcoming this by inviting them to talk to me about their nan or granddad, for example, and whilst they were talking I would write down what they were saying in a form that was readable. I then typed this up for them and usually included a significant picture of something their loved one was interested in or enjoyed – even if it was drinking! Having laminated it, I returned it to them so they could give it to their relatives and also keep a copy for themselves, which I often found in cells, festooned with rosary beads and a cross. I was sometimes amazed at the verbal fluency of some of these lads who could barely read or write, but once they felt deeply about someone could come out with amazing turns of phrase and expression of love. Still feeling a significant part of their family is immensely important to many of them although, by their own actions, they have often caused deep divisions in their relationships. But families themselves may also be difficult and unforgiving, and sometimes this makes matters worse. Kevin's mum died whilst he was in prison and he was allowed to attend her funeral. From another relative who was also in prison I gathered that family relationships were not too good, but I was horrified when

Kevin returned from the funeral absolutely broken, as when he had got there he was given an order of service which included all the names of the family on the front cover except for his. I asked to borrow it and took it home, where I scanned it into the computer and reprinted if for him with his name included and gave it back to him. His face was a picture and, unbeknown to me at the time, this had an amazing influence on his life. He got out of prison and I heard that he had started to attend a local church where he was doing well. The minister told me that he had kept that order of service and it always had pride of place on the top of the TV. Such a small action that meant so much.

Just as the chapel is the place for prisoners to attend automatically at a time of loss, so too staff come to us at times of remembrance. We hold memorial services not only for prisoners who have died whilst in our community, but also for members of staff who have died whilst in employment with us. We kept the format of the service virtually the same, whether prisoner or staff member, though personalised as much as possible. Many of the staff who died had been with us for a long time and were well known to many of us. Even one or two who had left the prison were still remembered by all in this way; a sign of the tremendous sense of community and teamwork that exists on the inside as we work together in our 'dark' place. Staff and prisoners also join together in the chapel for our annual Service of Remembrance, as both groups know ex-service members and have common experiences. Just before Christmas we have a Community Carol Service when we invite in local churches and other helpers to join together with the lads in celebrating the coming of Jesus. After the service, we serve mince pies and coffee and the congregation mingles freely. For some of the lads, this is a novel experience, and afterwards they say things like, 'Miss, that lady spoke to me', as though it is an unusual occurrence to be treated as a fellow human being. For our visitors too, it is a good experience as they see prisoners as they really are, and often how very talented they are too. I shall never forget the year a lad with a penny whistle enlivened our carol singing very much indeed!

Chapel has always been geographically and practically at the very heart of the prison. All the big meetings are held here, as it is the only space which can accommodate large numbers of people. For many years, it served as an ad hoc theatre where the lads would put on a short play for local youngsters to warn them of the effects of drugs and explain what prison is really like, in the hopes of deterring them from following that path. The chapel has at times hosted conferences and auditors, support groups such as AA and NA, and served as a filming area for prisoners making DVDs to send home to their families. All staff have access at any time, and a few will venture up there to pray or light candles at memorable times. Perhaps this typifies most poignantly the very essence of what Chaplaincy in prison is; it is always there, not 'in your face', not making demands, but quietly reminding people of sincere faith, and those with no apparent faith, that there is still a 'rumour of God'.

Over the years, we have not seen dramatic conversions in any number, but I believe that we have been planting seeds just by being there when people need us. God alone knows what happens to people when they leave prison, but our prayer is that every conversation or action of kindness, however brief and trivial, may one day be recalled and better understood. It has been our privilege to attend alongside so many people, all so different and yet each made in the image of God, and to share with them nothing of ourselves but, maybe, just maybe, a very small glimpse of the compassion and mercy of our loving Father God.

Pause for reflection

How does the 'man in the street' perceive God?
How do our lives reflect to others the knowledge of the faith that we have in God?
Do we offer our lives to God for Him to use?

Prayer

Father, thank You for all the people we meet every day. Father, many people are hungry to know You and yet do not know it, and may not know how to begin their search. Father, help us to 'live' You in all that we say and do, and be willing to share the life that You have given us. Amen.

CHAPTER 13

Seeking Wisdom and Understanding

Questions and comments from those looking for answers

'Ask and it will be given to you; seek and you will find; knock and the door will be opened to you.'

Matthew 7:7

Each prisoner is an amazing person, full of character and personality. There are certain prisoners, often those who have been in for a long time, who will exhibit the most profound depth of thought, with an element of humour, albeit sometimes a bit dark. Prisoners will often say exactly what they think. Francis told me he could paint better than Michelangelo: 'When I've had my Jack Daniels, I'm a Picasso!' Prisoners will ask questions that are honest as well as being profound.

I would hear very interesting and deep statements about the meaning of life as they see it. One lad commented, 'When I looked at the grafters, I saw people up to their eyes in debt on credit cards, so it was easier to be a drug dealer with easy money.' Another lad, who might have been described as a career criminal, expected to come to prison regularly to fund his lifestyle as 'an ordinary job doesn't pay enough'. When I asked how his children felt about this, he said that he had just bought his daughter her second new car – so they liked his lifestyle too! On a more sombre note, one lad just arriving in prison commented, 'Being in prison is like dying, without being dead.' Another said, 'Everyone wants to go to heaven, but no one wants to die.' He also had another pearl of wisdom: 'If God meant us to exercise, he would have put diamonds on the floor!' A youngster who I was challenging to give up his present way of life, startled me with the words, 'Asking me, Miss, to give up drugs, is like asking you to give up God. You like Him, don't you – just as I like drugs?'

The presence of a Chaplain is an invitation to questions about anything vaguely spiritual. Whilst some of the time it may just be a ploy to while away a few moments of inactive boredom, for the most part the questions are genuine. One is called to respond without warning to all sorts of inquiries about God. I have had to do more theological thinking on my feet in prison than anywhere else!

Many of the lads' questions are of a practical nature, for example, 'Where in the Bible does it say gambling is a sin?' and 'What does God think about tattoo parlours?' (This man had been rethinking his career plans and was seeking guidance.) My colleague was questioned on the matter of eternal life: 'On the Day of Judgment, will the fellow I hit come back with a black eye?' A memorable question came from a man who asked me, 'Is fate the same as religion?' His story was that he had run away from the police and hidden in a swamp so he wouldn't be seen by the police helicopter. As a result, he had suffered hypothermia and nearly died, so had ended up in hospital. Whilst there, the doctors discovered he had an undiagnosed heart condition, for which he was then able to receive treatment which actually saved his life. By contrast, a man who was in on a sex offence charge against his daughter asked, 'Was this free will or did God plan it?'

Often we are asked very hard questions, such as, 'Where does the soul go to?' and 'Why does God allow good people to die?' Some lads are really seeking to grapple with these issues, as many people do. Many lads come from backgrounds where they have received absolutely no spiritual instruction, so they come to us with a sort of naive freshness, without preconceived ideas. They really want to be given an answer that they can grasp and understand. Running a Bible study group with men such as this is very challenging and certainly a far cry from the more conventional groups that we experience in a church setting. I will never forget one comment: 'Why did God put the tree of life in the friggin' garden, anyway? It would have been a lot easier if He hadn't put it there...' Another time, someone asked, 'If all the people in the world were born onto a desert island, would evil ever get there?' A man, having watched part of the Alpha DVD, had questions such as, 'Which is better: a bad Christian or a good person?' We watched a DVD which had a story about two schoolfriends – one of whom became a judge and the other a burglar. They met again when the burglar was brought before the judge. The judge convicted the burglar, but then paid the debt himself. I was asked, 'But what about the victim [of the crime]?'

Sometimes the lads' questions and comments are somewhat negative about God, but often their hidden fears surface as they look for someone to blame for where they are and even who they are. Some of them admit to being scared by previous religious encounters and bad experiences of being 'forced' to believe. Others get confused with God and ghosts, and one lad said he wanted his cell 'blasting' because he felt 'someone else was in there'. Interestingly it was a cell where a previous occupant had taken his own life, and I was able to pray over it for him. Another lad thanked me for the Bible I had given to him and said that as a consequence he had just had the 'best night's rest' because it had sent him to sleep because it was so boring!

One of the most startling conversations was with a colleague of mine who was asked by a prisoner, 'Have you been speaking to the Big Fella?' Thinking that he meant the director of the prison, my colleague asked, 'Why?' The prisoner responded, 'Next time you speak to him, tell him he's a b******!' My colleague, quick-thinking, replied, 'Tell him yourself!' Prisoners' language is earthy and they 'say it as they find it'. The same colleague mentioned above was also assured by one lad that 'the f****** prayers worked'!

In spite of their foul language much of the time, many of them respect the presence of a Chaplain and the atmosphere in the chapel. Many spoke of the effect of being prayed for as 'a tingle' or 'when I prayed and lit a candle, all the evil came out'. They spoke of the chapel as 'a place of healing and peace'. Thomas told me that when he came to the chapel he always cried out, 'God forgive me!' and started to cry.

Although our contact with most of the men is fleeting, there is no doubt that they respond in some way to our offers of support and concern. One man came to speak to me because he said I had 'a caring voice', and another spoke of having his 'spirit lightened'. One sermon I preached had dramatic consequences. I was sent to see a lad who had attended the service and had subsequently been attacked on his unit. He said to me, 'It was because of what you said...' It transpired that I had preached on 'turning the other cheek', and he had literally done just that – and come off the worse for it! Their understanding of the spiritual is sometimes a bit hazy, but they clearly respond to something they can hardly articulate. A lad resident on Healthcare asked to receive communion as he had missed a service. He said that he wanted 'that thing in your mouth that dissolves and you bless me'. Even the courses we offer are esteemed by some. Howard, who had attended Living with Loss, thought it ought to go on *Dragon's Den*!

Even when released from prison, some lads come to appreciate the sanctuary of the church. One prisoner said that when he was last out he would go to the church to ask for water but never food, so they would not know he was homeless. I was asked by another lad to ring a local church to inquire about his clothes, which he claimed were under a bush in the cathedral car park. To my surprise, this was indeed the case, and he was well-known to the people there. Whatever a lad's faith or lack of it, the church was still esteemed by some. I was called over once by a man who told me he had decided to donate some money he was receiving from his family. He had asked for someone from the church because he wanted to send the money via them to a local foodbank. He felt that they would deal with the money responsibly.

There is no doubt that some do find faith in God or return to a latent belief whilst they are in prison. Usually this is in a rather 'unorthodox' way, as though God grabs their attention when they are not really expecting it. Amazing though it may seem, Paul told me that whilst he was on acid he saw a cross and he was on it, and so he became a Christian. Simon told me he was drunk for four days and was lying down on his couch at home. He tried to turn off the TV, but found the God Channel by accident and listened to the testimonies. As a consequence, he came off all drugs and went to church, but he was embarrassed because he kept slipping back into old behaviours. Back in prison, he cried out for help in understanding the reasons for his addictions, and got help for the first time in his life with mental health issues. Nick was on his way to meet his drug dealer and cut across a churchyard. He met a homeless man who told him he looked a mess and should go into the church. The people there gave him a meal of shepherd's pie and offered to pray with him. Nick repeatedly tried to ring his drug dealer, but each time he dialled it was engaged, and so he eventually accepted prayer. He went out with the people from church distributing leaflets which contained the words, 'There is no condemnation...' That message really touched him, and he said he felt 'like laying an egg'! When I prayed for him he admitted he hadn't prayed for ages and had 'forgotten the lyrics'.

Mark told me he found God in another prison whilst he was in CSU. In his words, in the middle of the 'cosmic darkness' he saw the word 'life' and the picture of a fruit tree, and he realised the fruit was God. Mark said he experienced God like 'a warm blanket'. Zac, also in CSU, was struggling with self-harm and a lot of mental health issues. I had given him a copy of 'Footprints', and a few days later he told me that God had picked him up and carried him, just as it said in the poem.

One might well ask why, if these conversions are valid, do many of these men end up returning to prison after they have been released. Does their faith really affect their lives? God alone can answer that question, but the fact that they share these experiences suggest that something has happened, which by God's grace may bring about the change they desperately need. Leon, a youngster, made the profound comment that 'God can change you and prayer makes you feel better'. John said he was glad he had come to prison because he had found comfort in the Bible.

As the saying goes, 'The proof of the pudding is in the eating.' If these lads really have made a commitment to God, they will display new attitudes and actions, both inside and outside jail. Often the most notable change is their attitude to forgiving others. One of the loveliest prayers I heard was composed by a man in his head who then dictated it to a friend to record on paper because he could not write himself. Ben wrote to his father asking for his forgiveness after reading a book on forgiveness; to ask this was a very significant step for Ben. Sometimes ideas still get a bit confused: Kevin sent a poem to his mother about forgiveness because he thought she needed to be forgiven for what she had done to him! However, the message that we need to get rid of the heavy burdens inside us that cripple all our relationships, is one which seems to resonate.

In prison, stripped of everything and with plenty of time to think, many prisoners who have had shreds of faith or spiritual experience in the past do sometimes reconnect with it. If youngsters have been taken to chapel, it will usually have been by grandparents, and we will hear that these family members are still praying for them. However awry the lads lives go, the memory of the faithfulness of grandparents never quite goes away. The lads come to a point of honesty with themselves and a willingness to change – the seed of their grandparents' faithfulness does bear fruit. A vivid memory I have is of speaking to Alan whilst he was in CSU. He was a very volatile prisoner and habitually self-harmed. During a previous encounter, he had told me how his father had taken him to church, but Alan had reacted violently to his mother's infidelity. He was terrified that he would never get out of prison, but underneath there was some response to spiritual truth. The conversation I had with him was through a hinge in his cell door, as I was not allowed to enter his cell due to the blood he had smeared round its walls. He was such a troubled man and yet, I saw as it were through the eyes of God, a frightened little boy, so in need of real love and compassion and, above all, healing of body, mind and spirit.

In the midst of the busyness of life, many people on the outside of prison scarcely give God a second thought. But, in the separate existence of prison, with nothing else to distract, no place to hide, there is an amazing amount of honest reflection. The vast majority prefer to decline spiritual support and wish to live their own lives in their own way, as do most people who have not been convicted of a crime. It is refreshing to meet people with no pre-conceived ideas who are asking questions that may be very difficult to answer. With no church background or spiritual learning, they come as they are, often with a penetrating lucidity and a need for answers which will satisfy their thirst for understanding. In conversation, they rarely come out with standard answers, and that in itself is refreshing. They really do want to learn and that, in itself, teaches them. Robert had attended chapel and Bible study groups regularly, but it was as he was studying the Emmaus course on his own that he suddenly saw Jesus as the Son of God and felt this was a new beginning. Only the Spirit of God convinces and convicts a person. No amount of head knowledge on its own can bring that about. Prisoners come simply and openly, and need to be able to respond in their own way and in

God's time. We, as Chaplains, see ourselves as those who sow the seed and leave the harvesting to the hands of God.

Pause for reflection

Do we have questions that we would like answered in a way that satisfies?
Are we prepared to admit our doubts about our faith to God?
How honest are we before God and others?

Prayer

Lord, thank You that You accept us just as we are, warts and all. Thank You that You came to find and save those who were lost, and You long for us all to know the assurance of Your purpose for our life. Give us all the gift of honesty and humility before You, so that as we come to You, stripped and broken, we may be more open to receive all that You long to pour into our lives. Amen.

CHAPTER 14

Holy Moments

Times of deep spirituality in prison

> For God, who said, 'Let light shine out of darkness,' made his
> light shine in our hearts to give us the light of the knowledge of
> God's glory displayed in the face of Christ.
>
> 2 Corinthians 4:6

Prison is a very dark place. And yet sometimes, in the blackness of existence inside, rays of hope do shine forth, and seem more beautiful as they lighten up their dreary surroundings. I learned so much myself from the prisoners, and was so uplifted on the occasions when I saw light in them, even though these were not necessarily spiritual awakenings. How can you measure the delight on the face of a prisoner who has achieved a certificate in basic education, and as you present it to him, he says, 'That's the first certificate I've ever had in my life, Miss.' Another prisoner, who was such a difficult lad and endlessly in trouble for aggressive behaviour, waved a piece of paper excitedly at me and pronounced the startling words, 'Miss, I've got a certificate to be a fryer!' My immediate thought was that he meant 'friar', and I wondered exactly what course he had been attending. Then the penny dropped as he added, 'I can get a job in a chippy now, as I'm leaving tomorrow!' The light in that boy's eyes will always remain with me as, for the first time in many weeks, he had seen a vestige of hope.

I saw that light again on the faces of Chinese prisoners who could speak very little English. We invited in a Chinese pastor who could communicate with them and understand their needs. Similarly, I saw it when Mohammed, who had been suicidal, was finally given a date for a deportation hearing from his solicitor. One of the most precious times is when we give Bibles to foreign prisoners in their own language; their faces shine!

Even with men who have committed serious crimes, there are moments that are awesome. I think of Peter, who could speak very little English when he first arrived, and who was struggling with guilt and flashbacks to a very unpleasant motoring offence that had led him to be incarcerated. Gradually, as his English began to develop, he began to come out of his shell. He was quite a burly man and had been a biker. So it came as a huge surprise when he asked me to come and see what he had made in his cell. He had used flour and water to make dough, which he had rolled out and then crafted the most exquisite roses, about a couple of centimetres long. This was extraordinary enough, but he had then painted these flour flowers, delicately tinting the extremities of the petals. The flowers were to make the most beautiful 'brooch'. I was so moved at this amazing beauty in such circumstances, and even more so when he presented some larger flowers to the chapel for use on the altar. Somehow this was a holy moment to me; a sense of the miraculous; a shaft of light breaking through. Did he have faith? Did he come to faith? I cannot say, but I believe that God was somehow at work in his life, and he certainly spoke to others through his offering to God.

In prison, creativity sometimes comes as a bit of a shock, and yet many of the prisoners do develop this side of their personality. The artwork they produce is often of the highest standard, and others create beautiful woodwork. Stephen, who was convicted of murder, discovered his artistic talent for the first time in prison. He was not very keen on attending education, but went to the art class. His first attempts were fairly mediocre, but then he began to achieve something quite remarkable. It was as though his feelings of remorse and regret were translated into his work, as he started to do pencil drawings of churches which were carefully composed of individual bricks, each one shaded with pencil. It took hours and hours to complete each drawing, but it was as though the therapy of 'colouring in' each brick was soothing. It was not surprising that he later won an award for his work – not surprising, except to him!

Mick told me he had been born in a brothel in Bolivia and had been given to missionaries by his mother because she thought they would give him a better life than she could. He went into the army where he told me he was trained to respond without thought to commands. In civilian life, he had witnessed a woman being abused by her partner and had reacted in the same way as he had been trained – without thought – and assaulted the abuser. He was a very interesting young man and someone discovered his artistic talent – he was skilled in topiary. His shaped bushes have provided a lasting memory and testimony to his stay with us. Beauty in dark places surely speaks to us of our creative God.

I have already spoken of the Living with Loss course and the revelations that came through speaking of bereavements and the associated struggles with our emotions. In spite of the fact that this course was not faith-based, there was such a sense of God's presence as we shared together, and we witnessed the light of understanding as lads saw themselves in a new way. More holy moments.

Sometimes the presence of God was awesome as we prayed for lads. Nearly always, from an earthly point of view, one was at a loss for words to give a person in deep distress, and one had to rely on the infilling of the Holy Spirit to speak out in faith. I was asked to go and see Peter, who was only in his forties yet had just been diagnosed with terminal cancer. The disease was advancing very quickly and he was unlikely to live for more than a few months. Understandably, he was very scared. His offence was against members of his own family and, as a consequence, he had no contact with anyone on the outside. Praying for inspiration, I went to see him in his cell and asked if he would like me to pray with him. He agreed, and so I prayed for peace and strength. When I finished, I looked up and saw tears streaming down his face, and I asked him what was wrong. His reply was, 'No one has ever prayed for me using my name before…' I felt humbled, and tried to explain that God knew him by name and loved him as an individual, whatever he had done in his life. I visited him again after that to pray with him, and when he was finally admitted to hospital, I went to visit him with a cross and a Testament. I found myself filled with compassion for him, although I was aware of the crimes he had committed. At that time, he was simply a fellow human being, close to death and very frightened. When he finally died, the prison was asked to take the funeral as there was no immediate family involvement. My colleague took the

service and I sat at the front of the chapel. The whole event was very poignant. As
we waited to go into the Chapel of Rest, the preceding funeral was ongoing. This
was for a beloved nan, and there were heaps of flowers and wreaths, and many
distressed relatives. Peter's funeral would be in stark contrast. The coffin arrived,
the cheapest type and completely unadorned. The only mourners were my colleague and myself. But, just as the service began, a few people came into the back
of the chapel. It transpired that they were in fact his family, which included his
victims. Words cannot express the confusion of emotions that I felt at that point. I
had got to know Peter quite well, as a dying man, and had felt God's love for him,
but now I was confronted by the evidence of his wrongdoing. The victims whose
lives had been so affected and would continue to be, by his actions. I found that
an indescribable moment of dichotomy which I could only commit to God as
my own understanding was so divided. Only God, in his infinite wisdom, could
understand. Maybe another very holy moment.

I started this chapter with the thought that we bring the light of Christ into
dark places. Because the light of Christ is within us, whatever happens, that
inner radiance is inextinguishable. One of the most amazing things a prisoner
said to me one night as I was going home was, 'There's the lady with the lamp.'
Without a moment's hesitation, I replied, 'That was Florence Nightingale!' The
response came, 'Well, you spread light around.' What an encouragement that
short sentence was. Yet, by the grace and with the strength of Christ it is true. On
so many occasions as I was speaking to lads, I was, humanly speaking, at a loss
for words. Sometimes I felt that anything I said would be irrelevant at the very
least, in light of the traumatic experiences they were recounting to me. And yet
I sometimes felt that God gave me just the right words at the right time; words
way beyond my wisdom. At other times, I felt overwhelmed with sorrow for them
and the compassion of God for them was quite overwhelming. If I stood back and
contemplated in my head just what they had done, I should have felt horror, fear
and probably revulsion, but it was as though God allowed me to feel through that,
with a deep understanding of the person and not the action and, in a miniscule
way, saw them as He did; as people whom He had made and loved. I always
kept with me the Gospel account of Jesus' encounter with the woman caught in
adultery. As her accusers slunk away, Jesus said, 'No more do I condemn you...'
But that is not the end. His next instruction was, 'Go and sin no more.' To me,

the two must always go together. Jesus does not condemn the person, but He does not condone the wrong that they, and all of us do. Above all, prison has reminded me of the extent of the grace of Christ and His work for us all on the cross, which covers over every kind of sin and rebellion.

I have two very vivid recollections of this fundamental truth really gripping me as I worked in prison. The first time came at the very first communion service I ever attended. It had been the practice that the priest would dispense the host and the prisoner was given the cup of wine to hold. For various reasons, we use the practice of intinction in prison, partly as this is considered more hygienic, but also because, if we allowed the prisoners to drink from the cup, the first one is liable to consume it all! So, I went forward to receive the bread and wine but, as I did, I looked up at the figure of Jesus that is suspended above the altar. It is a figure of the crucified, yet resurrected, Jesus and He has His arms outstretched in welcome. As I took communion, I was struck forcibly by the thought that 'We are all in the same place, below Jesus, at the foot of the cross.' In His sight, there is no 'pecking order' of priest, then me, then prisoner. At that moment, I saw in myself all my own anger, my own jealousy and my own bitterness and, above all, my own self-righteousness that made me think I was better than a prisoner. I saw that in me, as in all humans, there are the seeds of all the same things that makes a person commit a crime; all the things that separate us from our loving heavenly Father. As I was overwhelmed by the fact that I was forgiven by the grace of God through Christ, I cried. I began to see that no one can ever be outside the reach of God's grace and forgiveness, because Jesus came to die not for us at our best, but for us at our very worst. I was amazed recently to see that even St Paul saw himself as the lowest of the low and said, 'We have become the scum of the earth, the garbage of the world—right up to this moment' (1 Cor. 4:13). What interesting turns of phrase, as so often prisoners are referred to in this dehumanising way. I believe that no one is outside of God's great love for them as an individual, created in His image. Again I will say that I do not believe God condones the wrong things that we do, but I do not believe he condemns us either, but challenges us to stop doing wrong and begin to live our life in the way that He has ordained for us, by His strength at work within us.

This profound truth shaped the ministry that I exercised in prison. Time and time again, as I preached on the lectionary readings, that recurring theme seemed to be present. So perhaps it should not have been surprising that my last few months in prison were also blessed with something else that was connected to this truth. When we gathered for any service in the chapel, we usually always had a 'split' congregation. The main body of prisoners would sit at the front, but at the back we would have a separate row for those prisoners who were considered vulnerable. These come from the VP units, which normally house sex offenders, paedophiles and others who have committed crimes that other prisoners find unacceptable, such as harming old ladies or sometimes their girlfriends and partners. For security reasons, these prisoners never come into direct contact with the 'mains' because sometimes prisoners may take it into their own hands to deliver what they consider to be due punishment for these nonces. At all times, VPs are escorted through the prison by an officer, and they arrive in chapel through a back door so that they do not encounter the others. In some prisons, chapel services for VPs are completely separate from those for the 'mains' for this very reason, but we decided from the beginning that all those of faith should be allowed to worship together, but kept safe by being slightly separated. During communion, however, under the eyes of the officers, we allow the VPs to come forward with the other prisoners, and there has rarely been any problem with this. During the communion service, we also exchange the Peace, and by tradition the 'mains' have always shaken hands with each other, and the VPs likewise with each other. About six months before I left prison, we had a comparatively settled congregation who actually knew each other well. One day, one of the 'mains' went to one of the VPs during the time of the Peace and shook hands with him. I made no comment, but noticed that, as the weeks passed, a few more of the 'mains' followed his example. Some of the newer officers began to question whether this was OK, but we agreed that as it was not causing any problems, it was fine. Eventually, all the 'mains' were all shaking hands with the VPs, which is absolutely unheard of in prison culture. But something more happened. One day, I realised that not only were the prisoners shaking hands with each other, but they were also shaking hands with the prison officers – and that really is not normal! I just stood there, breathing in the scene and feeling acutely that this was indeed a 'holy moment' because only the presence of the living God could have effected such an amazing transformation of attitude. Just before I left, I was chatting with my group of VPs who attended a Bible study, and this sharing of the Peace came up. One of them said to me, 'It happened because of what you said…' I was completely taken aback and thought, 'But I deliberately never said anything either to encourage or discourage them from such a practice'. I knew that there were safety and security issues at stake, and I did not want to force anyone into feeling they had to respond in a certain way. But the lad added, 'You told us we were all the same…' I could only bow my head in humble acceptance of the mighty work of God that is abroad in moments such as these.

Maybe because prison is a place of such raw emotions, we have the privilege of 'seeing' God. A priest recently said to me that in many chaplaincy situations 'God is real'. Most of the encounters we have with the men are literally life and death situations, and human words alone can do little to ease their discomfort. Because it is so dark, the light of Christ is perhaps even more visible in these places. Stripped of their identity and their freedom, prisoners are perhaps more open to receive all that God longs to bring to every one of His children, whoever they are, and whatever they have done.

Pause for reflection

Do we recognise 'holy moments' in our lives, when we see God at work not only in ourselves, but in others?
How do we feel about the 'scum of the earth'?
Do we see others as God sees them, or do we use our own value judgements?
How can we view victim and perpetrator with the eyes of God?

Prayer

Father God, Creator of the universe, forgive us that sometimes we forget the greatness of who You are; that Your love far exceeds our experience, that Your wisdom far outweighs our understanding and Your grace really is all-sufficient for anyone and everyone. Help us to see others as You see them, in the light of Your compassion and grace. Amen.

CHAPTER 15

Throwing Away the Black Socks
Life after prison and support
of chaplains in prison

> Devote yourselves to prayer, being watchful and thankful. And
> pray for us, too, that God may open a door for our message, so
> that we may proclaim the mystery of Christ, for which I am in
> chains. Pray that I may proclaim it clearly, as I should.
>
> Colossians 4:2–4

My time for leaving the prison to retire finally came and, as I handed in my belt for the last time, I felt an enormous weight lift from me. The belt is heavy, as it carries a key pouch and a radio, but there was an emotional heaviness lifted as well. One of the first things I did after retirement was to throw away my black socks, which were worn as part of my uniform, in a symbolic gesture of breaking free!

Prison is an amazing place, and working there was very much a calling for me. It was also a privilege, because it allowed me to experience a very different way of life and to meet people who helped me not only to understand myself better, but also to reveal how my pre-conceived ideas, and even theology, had been based on a much more sheltered idea of life. It forced me to grapple with issues that I had previously not given much attention to or that had not been relevant to me and my way of life. My experience definitely changed me, hopefully for the better.

Why do prisons need chaplains? As we advance through the 21st century, with massive change and the secular world appearing to dismiss faith as almost irrelevant, why should we continue to be present in the hard world of prison? It is interesting that chaplaincy is still a statutory requirement, as religion is considered to be 'a good thing' even if it is not fully understood. It is still seen to be another strand in the rehabilitation process, as those with faith seem to have better resources to make good decisions. And yet the chaplaincy role is a very specific one, and I believe very much a specific calling. When one meets with fellow chaplains, we find that we have a great deal in common: we have to be strong and resilient, and above all have a very special heart for people of all types. A thoroughly pastoral ministry is not the calling for everyone, and the sheer number of people that we deal with on a daily basis, requires a special kind of understanding and wisdom. We are also working in a very formulaic type of environment, bound by rules and regulations, and we are managed by mainly secular people who also have to maintain and run a business. This may be quite different from the relatively autonomous positions within a parish run by Christians.

Sometimes it seems as if chaplaincy is considered in quite a different light to parish ministry, and yet both are callings to serve. Because chaplaincy is 'out there' in the middle of secular institutions, in some ways it does not conform to the normal pattern of priestly ministry. I did encounter the question as to whether it was necessary to be ordained to serve in prison. It was implied that ordination did not matter if one's ministry was mainly 'just' to listen and talk with people. I felt strongly that this person had missed the point. In my view, we need to continue to place ordained priests into prison, because with ordination comes the authority of the Church; the sealing of one's ministry with a mark of authentication. This does not mean that we seek power for ourselves, but rather that ordination is a sign of recognition of what we are doing. The dog collar is still understood to a degree by prisoners, and is very much respected. I must hasten to add that the role of lay people within the prison is also vital and not at all to be underestimated. If it was not for them, prison would be in a very poor place indeed.

However, I feel that whilst we still have an institutional church, as members of the Church of England we need to ensure that we continue to place priests inside prison. This is a ministry that is vital, and if we believe that God's grace reaches to all, we cannot exclude any part of our society, least of all the lowest of the low. As I shared the gospel with the lads, again and again I would be struck by the truth that Jesus' ministry was mainly itinerant, and not often in the synagogue. And also, the people to whom Jesus gave the most time were not the teachers of the law, but everyday people. They were the 'lowest of the low' in many cases, and yet Jesus did not shun them, but spent time with them – accepting them as they were at that time, but gently challenging them to move on into a fuller way of life. I sometimes used to speculate with the prisoners, 'If Jesus came back to earth tomorrow, do you think he would go to the church first, or come here?' Sometimes a light passed over their faces as they considered this, and realised that maybe Jesus might even pay them a visit. Even they might be thought to be 'visit-able'.

As priests, we are able to consecrate communion and share that sign of God's acceptance, not only of the 'great and good', but also of those who have fallen very far short of the glory of God. The deeper the transgression, so the deeper the love of Christ is seen in this act of forgiveness. To realise afresh that Christ's body was broken for the very greatest of sinners and that includes all of us individually, as our hearts are all 'desperately wicked', is to marvel again and again at exactly how amazing grace is. And prisoners do not take communion lightly. They have experienced being caught and found guilty in the law's sight, and are often so much more 'honest' about their own shortcomings than we are.

The other priestly act of blessing is also immensely important in prison. Very regularly, a prisoner would stop me and ask me for a blessing. Whilst, on many occasions, they may have been seen by the prisoner as a sort of good luck ritual, nevertheless it was interesting that many saw the significance of reaching out to a higher power, especially at times of stress and difficulty. There is something about the authority of priesthood that allows the strength of the blessing of God to reach another in a very special way. Time after time we were also asked to bless the 'rosemarys', and I would always say that I would pray a blessing on those who were wearing them. For many prisoners, the concept of someone praying for them personally seemed to be a new idea, but one that was very well accepted. There was always a very real sense for me of being a channel, being open to God and allowing His love to flow through me to the prisoner, in a way that defies human understanding or explanation.

So how does chaplaincy, specifically prison chaplaincy, fit in to the local church context? How can we be part of the local worshipping community and yet at the same time minister in an entirely different environment? In many ways prison chaplaincy could be seen as equivalent to the 'Fresh Expressions' initiative in the local church – a type of pioneer ministry, reaching people where they are, rather than meeting them primarily when they attend chapel. We not only minister to the de-churched, but to those who have never been anywhere near or a church and may have very negative and even destructive attitudes towards it.

In a multi-cultural society, we have very specific guidelines about any kind of proselytisation and so, whilst we preach the gospel day in and day out, it is often simply through the compassion and care that we give to individuals. Above all else, it is about the non-judgmental acceptance of prisoners as individuals who are of worth in themselves – that is the raison d'être for all we do. We are dealing daily with really raw emotions and 'edge of the cliff' situations, and we have to react and advise in a very short time. It is very much done on 'a wing and a prayer', and most of what we say is probably 'sanctified common sense'. But there is a tremendous sense that we are with needy, and therefore receptive, people all the time. Whatever the outcome of our conversations with them, we have in some respects touched their lives, and as we believe that through us that touch is from God, it is a massive privilege. I was always overawed when prisoners said to me that something that I had said without preparation, had had an impact on them. Did they find God in a real way and change their lives as a consequence? Sadly, I suspect there will be a lot further to go with many of them, as the complexity of their upbringing and the baggage that most of them carry is something that may need to be worked at gradually. In the vastness of the job we were challenged with every day, we appreciated that many of our encounters were like those on the road to Emmaus: a partial and fleeting encounter, part of a journey, a seed sown that may one day bear fruit. I do not believe any conversation was wasted, and one can only leave to God the final outcome. But I do believe that if there were no chaplains in prison, there would be something missing. We are so privileged that we are still considered useful enough to remain, and not be an additional extra at the whim of suitable funding.

When I was attending some initial training for chaplaincy work, we were told that as chaplains we had three roles in prison: as priests, pastors and prophets. The function of prophet was to be seen in serving as a 'conscience' in the prison; to be there and to be able to comment and participate in managerial decisions to ensure the health and safety of all. Whilst our status in the hierarchy of the prison system has been downgraded over the years, nevertheless we are still in that vital place of being in the centre of things and available for all. However, this is not always a very comfortable position to be in, especially as we understand only too well the ground-floor-level stresses whilst also seeing the requirements that the whole system needs to deliver. We need so much prayer to contribute graciously and wisely, and yet are grateful that we are in this position, as independent and neutral ministers of God's Word with the authority of the Church.

So how can the established Church help those who are called to minister as prison chaplains? Above all, every chaplain appreciates support and prayer. Our ministry is at a distance from the parish, and does not operate in the same way, and so requires understanding. I was extremely grateful for a member of my own congregation who simply listened to me as I shared my feelings of having to break the news to the respective families of three lads who had committed suicide. They had all died within the space of just over a month. I hardly knew myself what I was feeling, but as I was listened to, I felt so much better. Most of the situations we encounter in prison cannot be discussed outside its walls, and this also puts pressure on the chaplains as they are left to absorb things. As a team, we debrief each other, and very early on I learnt to put an imaginary 'lace curtain' between me and the prisoner so, whilst I continued to empathise with him, I did not take the heaviness of the emotional burden onto myself. But, as the years go by, emotional and spiritual resources do become depleted, and it is vital that this is understood and there is an appropriate support system available. Support for chaplains is difficult because their work style is very different to that in a parish. Whilst we have a reasonably fixed daily schedule and therefore tend not to work on into the evenings, our days are extremely concentrated and, as mentioned before, every encounter tends to literally concern a 'life or death' situation. The latter far exceed the former! Nearly all the news we take to prisoners is under the heading of 'bad', and nearly everyone with whom we engage is in the midst of some sort of crisis. There is very little remission for us!

Added to this, we are also part of the prison institution and, as such, have to conform to their requirements. This involves having annual appraisals from a 'business' perspective. It is very hard to justify what we do in their model of achievement. We are recognised in our capacity to 'care' and to be available, and our value is understood by nearly all the staff, but it is still hard to be assessed by people who are not necessarily of faith, and to set our yearly targets with them. Tying this back into the church's system of appraisal is also extremely difficult, because chaplains are very much in the minority in numerical terms, and the appraisal system needs to be most appropriate for those in parish ministry. On a personal level, I very much appreciated meeting up with a local priest from time to time, not to be assessed, but to have a meal together, when we could just chat together about our respective ministries. In itself, this was encouraging; just to know that ministers on the outside cared and were interested in what was happening inside. Because of the peculiar nature of prison chaplaincy, the other support has been in fellow chaplains meeting together to discuss 'inside' stories and start with a mutual understanding. Unfortunately, due to spending cuts, such meetings are now infrequent and this has removed a significant part of our support system.

We do long for churches to pray for us and simply to be aware of the ministry that is active outside the church doors in the part of the community that we serve. It is relatively easy to pray for 'worthy' causes such as hospitals and schools, but prisons tend to be omitted. It is easy to feel that prisoners are inside due to their own actions, without remembering again that they are still individuals very much in need of God's care and forgiveness. Prison is an uncomfortable place to think about because it throws up such conundrums of theology, and sometimes forces us into changing our own worthy preconceived ideas.

As I have worked in the penal system, I have come to the conclusion that prison in itself is almost a signpost to the future of society as a whole. By this I mean that prison is a microcosm of the world around us and of society in general. It is a concentration of the worst parts of society; the deepest depths of what is possible.

It is as though the people who come to prison show us the problems in society, before they reach public attention. We were instructed about extremism and radicalisation years before those words entered society's common vocabulary. We also see the growing effects of dysfunctional families and the need for 'belonging' to a gang culture and its increasingly violent consequences. We witnessed for several years the horrendous influence of NPSs and other substances whilst they were still 'legal highs', several years before they were discussed on the outside community, and finally legislation was changed.

If we want to see where society is going, we need to look at the changing face of prison and its community. I have described in detail the brokenness of so many lives and, whilst they may be patched up, the damage can never be permanently undone. I have described too the difficulties of getting back into the outside world, only to go back into the same environment that put people behind bars in the first place. Over the past few decades, our society has changed greatly and the speed of change has been monumental. The whole attitude to life in general has shifted to a 'me culture' that seeks materialistic and hedonistic gratification, and demotes the needs of others. Or, at worst, sees others as an irrelevance. The loss of respect for anyone in authority, and the growing absence of appropriate fear of any consequences, accounts for much of the behaviour, especially amongst the youngsters of today. How this will affect future generations is difficult to know, but the already dysfunctional family producing more dysfunctional youngsters who carry on in the same way, makes for gloomy predictions. I cannot but equate these changes to the loss of 'godliness', and the fact that belief in any kind of god has waned. Our society has become more liberal with its attitudes to all sorts of things, and the structure of discipline has slackened. The result is generations of youngsters who really have no clear structure and hence are easily led astray. There is no 'easy fix' for this situation, but we need to be praying earnestly for future generations. I do believe that if there was a turn again to the living God, that we might see many attitudes changing.

I have been so privileged to share in the ministry of prison chaplaincy over the years. I stand back amazed as I recall the sense of somehow sharing in the ministry of Christ to those who are in the 'wrong' place. Someone once said to me that they found it easy to see the 'face of God' in those who have been born with disabilities, but that it was harder to see the same in prisoners. I found I could not agree with that because, in so many ways, I feel that I have met with God through these prisoners in a way that is beyond understanding. As I have shared with these fellow travellers I thank God for all the prisoners I have met and who have shared their stories, because it has helped me to find again that sense of awe at just how wide and deep and high is God's love and forgiveness, and the change that is possible in Him. I will always remain part of that life through my memories and the compassion I continue to feel through the grace of Christ for all. No one is outside the extent of His mercy and forgiveness.

Pause for reflection

How do we honestly feel about people in prison?
Do we believe that God can change prisoners' lives?
Do we sometimes put ourselves into a 'prison' of sadness and regret?
How can we be part of bringing in God's kingdom closer to all on earth?

Prayer

Loving Father, we come You just as we are, with all our weaknesses and strengths. Thank You that You meet us where we are, with open arms, not judgment or conditions. Help us to pray for every one of Your created children, especially for those who have got life so wrong. Fill us with Your compassion and an understanding of Your love, so that we can respond to others with this same compassion and love. Amen.

Acknowledgements

I would like to thank all my colleagues who walked alongside during my time in prison and shared with me in heartbreak, hope and holy moments.

I would like to thank all the Staff at Waverley Abbey Resources who have been so wonderfully helpful and supportive of my first journey into publishing.

I would like to thank my wonderful husband and sons for always being there and supporting me every step of the way.

Learn to be the Difference

We help people to develop their gifts, be equipped and make a difference.

We provide training in the areas of

- **Counselling**
- **Leadership**
- **Spiritual Formation**
- **Chaplaincy**

Courses that equip you to be the difference

WAVERLEY ABBEY
COLLEGE

Contemporary Chaplaincy – One Year

This course is designed to equip those serving or looking to serve in a broad range of community or church-based settings.

waverleyabbeycollege.ac.uk

PRISONS WEEK
A WEEK OF PRAYER

Prisons Week equips and enables the Church to pray for all those affected by prisons: prisoners and their families, victims of crime and their communities, those working in the criminal justice system and the many people who are involved in caring for those affected by crime on the inside and outside of our prisons. Prisons Week produces resources and provides an annual focus and reason for Christians to unite together in prayer that moves the heart of God to action.

Prisons Sunday – the second Sunday in October – marks the beginning of the week of prayer each year, running through until the following Saturday.

For more information visit **www.prisonsweek.org**

9 781789 514285